THE PRACTICAL
GARDENING
ENCYCLOPEDIA

THE PRACTICAL
GARDENING
ENCYCLOPEDIA

Peter McHoy

Colour Library Books

CLB 4227

This 1994 edition first published for
Colour Library Books Ltd
Godalming Business Centre
Woolsack Way
Godalming
Surrey GU7 1XW

© Anness Publishing Limited 1994
Boundary Row Studios
1 Boundary Row
London SE1 8HP

ISBN 1-85833-138-2

Editorial Director Joanna Lorenz
Project Editor Jennifer Jones
Photographer Paul Forrester
Designer Michael Morey
Illustrator Kate Simunek

Typeset by MC Typeset Limited

Printed and bound in Hong Kong

CONTENTS

GARDENING BASICS 9

FLOWERS & FOLIAGE 93

FRUIT & VEGETABLES *171*

GARDENING BASICS

A garden does not look after itself, and if you
want to get the best from your plants you have to
think about the basics like watering, feeding,
weeding, and pest and disease control.
Fortunately, as the following pages show, these
need not become onerous chores . . . and they are
well offset by the delights to be discovered in the
more 'creative' aspects of gardening such as
propagation. Even pruning can be creative, as you
learn to shape the shrubs as well as improve their
flowering.

OPPOSITE
Propagation is one of the most satisfying
aspects of gardening, and if you have a
greenhouse the scope is widened
enormously.

INTRODUCTION

Gardening is a practical hobby that combines the art of design and the creative use of plants with the science of horticulture and the mechanics of garden construction. The following pages will help you to build a better garden and to keep your plants growing healthily.

Using the right tools always makes gardening easier, and whether you are just beginning to garden or have been growing plants for years and simply want to replace an old tool, the advice on choosing tools will get you off to a good start.

Adequate ground preparation is something that beginners in particular overlook, yet it can spell the difference between success and failure. In the following pages you will find hints and tips on testing and improving your soil, and advice on how to make good garden

ABOVE A weed-free lawn is as easy as watering, if you use one of the modern selective hormone weedkillers.

compost . . . something that even experienced gardeners can find difficult to achieve.

Few plants will thrive without feeding and watering, and there are plenty of practical know-how tips to take the mystique and hard work out of both chores.

Pests and other problems are part of gardening. Even the most expert gardener gets them. You will find simple no-nonsense advice on how to deal with some of the most common problems, with an organic solution as well as a chemical approach wherever appropriate.

Propagation is not only money-saving, it's fun and very satisfying. You will find all the major propagation techniques described in easy-to-follow steps, with a section on special or unusual techniques for those who like to try something a little different.

ABOVE Even paving stone paths can be interesting if you use your imagination and mix materials. Here, beach pebbles are being used to vary the texture.

LEFT Hand weeding still has a place, especially close to other plants.

LEFT A sawn log path, surrounded by chipped bark, makes an attractive path for a wild part of the garden.

BELOW Lawns benefit from a neat, crisp edge, and proprietary lawn edging strips do the job well.

Pruning is perhaps the one task that newcomers – and even many experienced gardeners – tackle with the most trepidation. The section on pruning removes the mystique by reducing the problem to a few common-sense steps that will cover the majority of shrubs.

Whether you are starting a garden from scratch or adding to an existing one, perhaps by building a patio or pergola, some construction work is inevitable. Even if you are a newcomer to it, you will find here all the information you need for basic garden construction jobs.

ABOVE, CENTRE Keep on top of pests and diseases, especially with plants prone to them, such as roses.

ABOVE Propagation can be as simple as pegging down a shoot on those plants that can be layered.

LEFT Routine pruning will keep shrubs such as roses in good shape and flowering well.

CHOOSING TOOLS 1:
DIGGING AND CULTIVATING TOOLS

The right tools really do make a difference. A good quality, well-designed tool will often make a job much easier and will help to take the hard work out of gardening.

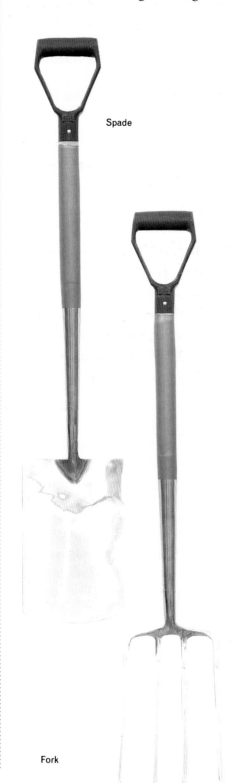

Spade

Fork

SPADES

Choose a spade with a long handle if you are tall. If you can afford it, a stainless steel spade will make digging easier.

◾ A D-shaped hilt provides a good grip – but make sure that you can get your hand in easily when wearing a gardening glove.

◾ Choose a full-sized blade if you have a lot of digging to do, but if you want a spade only to cultivate established borders or to plant trees and shrubs, a border spade with a blade of about 23 × 13cm (9 × 5in) may be more useful.

◾ A tread on top of the blade makes it less tiring on the feet when you push the spade into the ground, but the spade will be a little heavier as a result. Stainless steel spades do not have treads.

◾ A wooden shaft is strong and comfortable to hold. Metal shafts should be coated with plastic.

Left: special trowel designed to fit onto separate handle as part of a range of tools. Centre: traditional hand trowel and fork. Right: narrow trowel, useful for a rock garden

FORKS

A garden fork can be used instead of a spade for digging on heavy clay soils, but it is also invaluable for lifting bulky material such as manure and garden compost.

◾ A D-shaped hilt is generally stronger than a Y-shaped one, and more widely available than T-shaped hilts. Make sure that you can fit your hand in easily when wearing a gardening glove.

◾ For general cultivation and lifting, choose a full-sized head with square prongs.

HOES AND RAKES

A hoe is one of the basic gardening tools, vital if you want to keep down the weeds. If you want one hoe, go for the Dutch type.

◾ The Dutch hoe is excellent for weeding between rows and around plants. Its angled head is designed to slice through weeds with the

Left: weeding trowel. Centre: patio/paving weeder. Right: daisy grubber

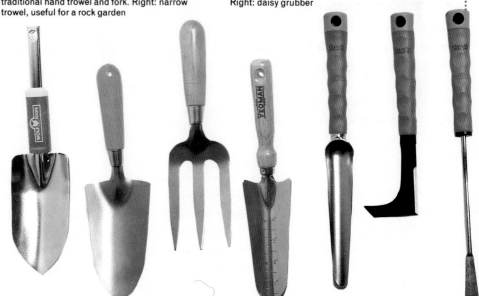

Left: draw hoe. Centre: proprietary three-bladed hoe. Right: Dutch hoe

Hand cultivator head that can be fitted to a long or short proprietary handle

minimum damage to plant roots. The wider the head, the quicker the weeding, but a narrow head is easier to use among plants.

∎ Choose a long handle so that you have less bending to do.

∎ An angled end and moulded grip make the tool easier to use.

∎ A draw hoe has an angled head that is useful for taking out flat-bottomed drills for seeds (use the corner for a normal drill), and for drawing up earth around crops such as potatoes. You can also use it to weed with a chopping motion.

∎ Patent hoe designs sometimes have a smaller blade that cuts on more than one side for working close in among plants.

A rake is most useful in a kitchen garden where you need to level the soil regularly, and when making a new garden.

∎ Choose a long handle so that you have less bending to do.

∎ Buy a head that is made in one piece. Riveted heads are not so strong. The wider the head, the more quickly you can rake an area, but balance this against the extra weight involved.

HAND CULTIVATORS AND WEEDERS

Hand cultivators are useful for breaking up the ground after digging, and for weeding between and along rows of seedlings or small plants, but are less efficient than a hoe for this task.

∎ A cultivator that has removable prongs is more versatile than a fixed-prong type, especially when working among plants.

∎ Choose one with a long handle. A handle that can be used with other heads and accessories is useful.

Special tools are available for grubbing out daisies and other weeds in a lawn, and others are designed for weeding among paving. These are useful, but worth buying only if you have a regular use for them.

HAND FORKS AND TROWELS

Trowels are inexpensive and indispensable – you will need them for planting, but they are also useful for weeding and filling pots and containers with compost.

You can manage without a hand fork, but it is useful for weeding and loosening soil.

∎ A wide-bladed trowel is best for planting and general use around the garden. A stainless steel blade is well worth the extra money you will pay, as it will not rust and should last much longer.

∎ A narrow blade is useful for working in confined areas, such as a rock garden.

∎ When buying a hand fork, make sure that the prongs are strong and the head is firmly fixed to the handle part.

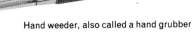

Hand weeder, also called a hand grubber

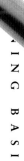

Left: conventional rake. Above: a proprietary rake design

CHOOSING TOOLS 2: MOWERS

Almost every gardener owns a mower, but it is important to choose the most appropriate type for your garden.

WHICH MOWER?

Manual mowers are worth considering for a very small lawn.
Side-wheel mowers without a roller attachment are the lightest and easiest to use.
Rear-roller mowers are the best choice for a small lawn if you want a striped finish.
Wheeled rotary electric mowers are the first choice for a lawn of modest size if you do not require a striped finish. For a large lawn, where trailing cables could be a problem, a petrol cylinder mower is a better and safer choice.
Hover rotary mowers – electric or petrol – are useful for cutting awkward places, such as beneath low overhanging branches, and shallow slopes. They are light and easy to manoeuvre.

Although rotary mowers do not usually have rear rollers to produce stripes or grass boxes to collect grass, this is not always the case – models are available that have both of these features. Shop around to see what is available at the time you want to buy.

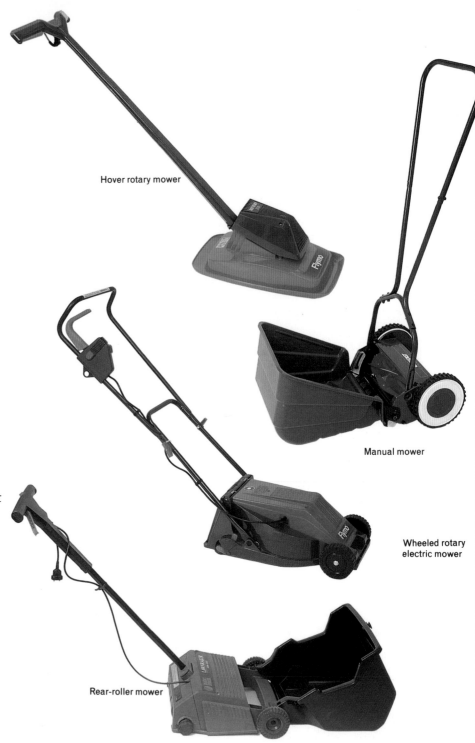

Hover rotary mower

Manual mower

Wheeled rotary electric mower

Rear-roller mower

SHARPENING

You can sharpen mower blades yourself, especially those of rotary mowers, but it is best to have them done professionally. Rotary mower blades are not expensive to replace. Some models can be fitted with plastic safety blades, and you may want to consider using these.

ELECTRICAL SAFETY

Check the cables and plugs on electric mowers for damage or loose connections. Always do this at the beginning of each season, but do not be complacent between-times. If your house wiring is not fitted with an earth leakage circuit breaker (or residual current device), buy a special power point which has one fitted. You can then use it for all your electrical gardening equipment.

Always brush or wipe the blades clean after mowing. Remove any accumulations of mowings noticed on other parts of the mower. *Always disconnect the power supply before cleaning an electric mower*.

Adjust the cutting height periodically to suit the time of year and rate of growth of the grass. Cut high in the spring, and then gradually reduce the height. The adjustments on your cylinder mower may

not be the same as the mower illustrated – consult the manufacturer's handbook. Rotary mowers can also be adjusted for height of cut. Consult the manufacturer's manual for the correct method.

Adjust the blades of a cylinder mower so that it cuts cleanly and evenly along the length of the blade. Use a sheet of paper to check that it cuts cleanly along the length of the blade. Rotate the cylinder slowly and carefully as you move the sheet of paper along the length of the cylinder.

If the paper does not cut cleanly along the length of the blade, make the necessary adjustment to the blade setting. Your mower may work on a different principle, so consult the handbook for your particular machine.

At the beginning of the season, and every month or two afterwards, put a drop of oil on bearings and chains. This will make the mower much easier to push.

WINTER WORK

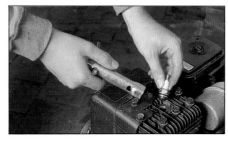

Drain the petrol and oil from a petrol mower before you put it away for the winter.

Clean and adjust or replace the spark plug. Check your handbook for the appropriate gap setting.

Before replacing the spark plug, pour a tablespoonful of oil into the cylinder. Then pull the starter to turn the engine over about half a dozen times before replacing the spark plug.

Wipe the mower with an oily rag, or spray with an anti-rust aerosol, before storing.

Before storing a rotary petrol or electric mower, clean the metal blades with an emery cloth.

Wipe the blade over with an oily rag to reduce the risk of rusting. If the blade is in poor condition, replace it with a new one.

CHOOSING TOOLS 3: TRIMMING AND PRUNING TOOLS

After cutting the lawn, hedge-trimming is one of the most labour-intensive and boring jobs in the garden. Electric hedge-trimmers make light work of the task, but hand shears may be preferable for a short hedge or trimming an individual shrub.

HEDGE-TRIMMERS

The longer the cutting length of a hedge-trimmer, the more quickly you will cut the hedge. The longest blades are usually found on heavy machines, however, and petrol-powered hedge-trimmers in particular are tiring to use. A 40cm (16in) blade is suitable for a small or medium-sized garden, but if you have a large garden with a lot of hedges, a 60cm (24in) blade will save a lot of time.

■ A double-sided cutting edge is useful if you like to cut with a sweep in both directions, but many gardeners use hedge-trimmers with a sweep in one direction only.

■ If both blades move (rather than one moving blade cutting against a stationary blade), vibration is likely to be much less. This is called a reciprocating action.

Hand shears

■ The more teeth there are for a given length of blade, the finer the finish is likely to be – but widely spaced teeth cope better with very thick shoots.

■ Blade extensions that project beyond the cutting blades reduce the risk of injury. These are also described as blade guards.

■ A hand shield should always be included with the hedge-trimmer.

■ A lock-off switch, which requires two separate actions to turn on the machine, makes accidental starting less likely.

CHOOSING HAND SHEARS

Hand shears, also called hedging shears, must be kept sharp, and the pivots or bearings oiled regularly to reduce the amount of physical effort required.

■ Make sure that the blades are easy to adjust. If too slack they will not cut properly; if too tight they will be hard to use.

■ Most shears have straight blades. These with wavy blades tend to cut through hard shoots more easily, but sharpening them is difficult.

■ A thick-shoot notch in the blade is useful if you have to cut through

Hedge-trimmer with double cutting edge and blade guards

GARDENING BASICS

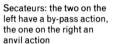

SECATEURS

■ Anvil secateurs cut when a sharp blade slicing through the stem is held against a flat anvil (usually made of a softer material). The anvil sometimes has a groove in it to allow the sap to run away. Anvil secateurs are likely to crush or tear the stem if the blade is not kept well sharpened.

■ By-pass secateurs have a scissor-like action, and are more likely to produce a sharp, clean cut than anvil secateurs.

■ Brightly coloured handles make the tool easier to see if you put it down whilst working.

■ The safety catch should be convenient and easy to use.

■ Make sure that the spring does not hold the blades open too wide or offer too much resistance to allow for a comfortable grip.

Secateurs: the two on the left have a by-pass action, the one on the right an anvil action

LONG-HANDLED PRUNERS

You will find these sold under a variety of names, such as loppers and branch cutters, but they all do the same job: cut through shoots and branches too thick for ordinary secateurs, and make reaching within a shrub much easier.

■ By-pass blades may be easier to manoeuvre into a confined space.

■ The longer the handle, the more leverage you will have and the less effort required to cut through a thick branch.

Long-handled pruners, sometimes called loppers

a thick shoot and you don't have secateurs to hand.

■ Handles are less important than the blades. Their shape and the material they are made from have little bearing on the ease with which the shears are used.

Tree pruner

CHOOSING TOOLS 4: OTHER USEFUL TOOLS

As well as the traditional garden tools there are newer ones designed to do specific jobs, such as shredding garden waste or raking moss from lawns. Some of the most useful ones are described here.

NYLON-LINE TRIMMERS

Nylon-line trimmers are the modern equivalent of the traditional scythe, but they are far more versatile and useful.

Use them to trim long grass around trees or right up to the edge of a fence or wall (difficult to do with a mower), or for chopping down weeds. More powerful machines with stronger cutters (sometimes metal discs) are called brushwood cutters; these are suitable for tough undergrowth.

■ A cutting guide will keep the spinning line off the ground and prevent it scalping the ground.
■ Two handles are needed to control a trimmer easily, and an adjustable shaft handle makes manoeuvring easier.
■ An automatic or semi-automatic line feed is useful as the line soon wears away.
■ A swivel head is useful if you want to use the trimmer to edge a lawn. It's easier than trying to hold the whole tool at an angle.

SHREDDERS

Shredders are useful if you like to recycle as much garden refuse as possible, but their cost is usually justified only if you have a lot of material to shred.

Shredders chop or mash woody and soft material so that it rots down more easily on the compost heap.

■ The outlet spout should be high enough off the ground to slide containers beneath it easily. Sack holder clips are useful for collecting material in sacks.

Electric shredder

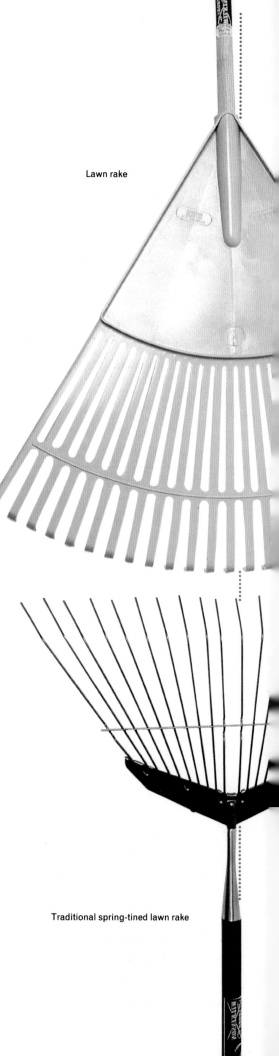

Lawn rake

Traditional spring-tined lawn rake

Half-moon edgers, sometimes called edging irons

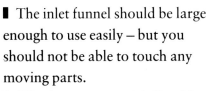

■ The inlet funnel should be large enough to use easily – but you should not be able to touch any moving parts.

■ Wheels are very useful. Shredders are heavy, and electric shredders cannot be left outside unprotected. One without wheels is satisfactory if you are able to use it where it is stored, but make sure that the legs are sturdy and stable.

LAWN RAKES

Lawn rakes are useful for raking out moss and 'thatch' (the dead grass and debris that forms around the base of the grass plants) from a lawn. They are also useful for scattering worm casts and raking up autumn leaves.

■ There are many kinds of manual lawn rakes, but the traditional fan-shaped spring-tined rake is one of the most useful. It is light and easy to use, and works well.

■ Powered lawn rakes save a lot of effort if you have a large lawn. They also have the benefit of collecting the leaves, moss and general debris as you work.

■ The wider the machine, the more expensive it is likely to be, but for a large lawn the saving in time will make it worthwhile.

EDGING TOOLS

If you have a large lawn with a lot of edges, a half-moon edger (also called an edging iron) could be useful. It is used against a straight-edged piece of wood (one foot on the wood to steady it, the foot pressing on the tool) to straighten an uneven edge.

Although useful, over-use will gradually make your lawn smaller and beds and borders bigger!

Use long-handled edging shears or a nylon-line trimmer with a swivel head to trim grass that simply overhangs the edge.

If the edge keeps getting broken down, buy a metal or plastic edging strip to reduce the problem.

Nylon line trimmer

Preparing The Ground 1

Digging helps to aerate the soil and expose pests to predators, and gives you the chance to incorporate humus-forming manures or garden compost. For heavy clay soils it can also help to improve the structure. The autumn and early winter is the best time for digging, but you can finish it off in the spring.

SINGLE DIGGING

1 If you have a large area to dig such as a vegetable plot, or a new garden to cultivate, divide it into two equal areas. Then you can dig to one end and work back down the other side to finish where you began.

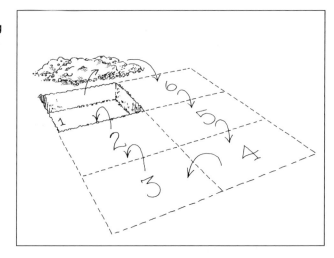

2 **ABOVE** Remove a trench the width and depth of a spade, and pile up the soil at the end of the bed.

3 **ABOVE RIGHT** Drive the spade into the soil at right angles, and no more than a spade's width away from the previous 'bite' of soil. Push the spade in as far as possible without having to kick it in.

4 **RIGHT** Push the spade in parallel to the trench, taking a bite about 15–20cm (6–8in) deep. Do not take larger bites otherwise they will be heavy to lift. If necessary use your foot to press the spade fully into the ground.

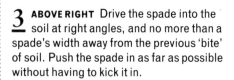

GARDENING BASICS

5 Pull back on the handle, using it as a lever to loosen the bite of soil, which will pull free on to the blade.

6 Lift the bite of soil, keeping your back as straight as possible and doing the lifting with your knees, and flick the soil over with a twist of the wrist. Inverting the clods of soil will bury the weeds. When you have reached the end of a row, work back in the opposite direction. To remove the first bite from each row, make two slices at right angles before inserting the spade between them parallel to the trench.

7 When you reach the end of the plot, fill the last trench with soil from the first row of the return half.

8 When you have dug the last row, fill in the trench left with the soil excavated from the first trench.

DIGGING A SMALL AREA

For a small area of ground in the garden, don't bother to divide the area or to remove the initial trench. Just throw the soil forward slightly as you work, then rake it level when preparing the ground for sowing or planting.

PERENNIAL WEEDS

If the soil is inverted properly, most annual weeds will be killed and will decompose to add humus to the soil. Remove the roots of troublesome perennial weeds by hand to prevent their spread.

USING A GARDEN FORK

Use a spade for normal digging, but choose a fork to loosen ground that has already been dug recently and simply needs aerating, or where persistent perennial weeds are a problem. A fork is less likely to slice through the roots to leave pieces behind, and by shaking the soil through the prongs it is easier to remove troublesome weeds.

Loosen the roots with a garden fork.

Pull up the roots by hand.

PREPARING THE GROUND 2

Whether planting or sowing seeds, you need to break the soil down to a fine tilth (structure) first after digging to open it up and remove weeds. Fine, crumbly soil is essential if you are sowing seeds, and for a lawn or an area where appearance is important, you may need to level the surface too.

PRODUCING A FINE TILTH (STRUCTURE)

1 Remove any large weeds that have been missed when digging, or that have started to grow since. Be especially careful to pull out completely the roots of pernicious weeds that grow and spread if just a few are left behind.

2 If the initial digging was done in the autumn and you are sowing or planting in the spring, go over the ground with a fork to turn in weed seedlings that have germinated, and to open up the soil again.

LEVELLING WITH PEGS

1 Prepare a supply of pegs about 15cm (6in) long. Paint or mark a band all round each peg, about 12–25mm (½–1in) from the top. It is not critical which distance you choose, but it is important that each peg is marked in exactly the same position.

2 Level the ground roughly by eye first, then insert a row of pegs about 1m (1yd) apart, using a known level surface as a reference point if possible. Push the pegs in so that the painted mark is at soil level.

3 Insert another row of pegs 1m (1yd) away from the first row. Use a long spirit-level (or a shorter one on a straight-edged piece of wood) to make sure that the pegs in each row are level. Check each peg in more than one direction, and adjust the height of the pegs as required.

4 Once each row of pegs has been levelled accurately, go on to the next row. Repeat the process until the area has been pegged. Rake the soil level, making sure that it comes up to the same position on each peg.

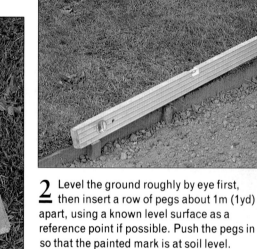

3 A hand cultivator like the one shown here is useful for breaking down large clods of earth and doing some of the initial levelling. Use it with a pulling motion.

4 Use an ordinary garden rake for the main levelling and smoothing, raking first in one direction and then the other.

5 You can use a combination of hoe and rake to produce a very fine soil structure for a seed bed, but a tool like this star-wheeled cultivator will make the job easier. Pushing it to and fro will break down the soil to make it fine and crumbly.

Seeds need a light, fine soil if they are to flourish.

TESTING YOUR SOIL

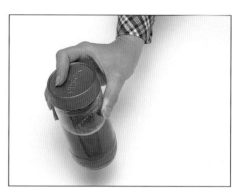

You can't determine how acid or alkaline your soil is, or how rich or deficient in nutrients, just by looking at it. Fortunately, simple and inexpensive soil-testing kits will give you quick results without the time or expense of a proper laboratory test. However, none of the do-it-yourself kits described here are as accurate as using a soil test laboratory, but they are better than nothing.

TESTING FOR MAJOR NUTRIENTS

1 Gather your soil sample, using a trowel, from 5–8cm (2–3in) below the surface. Take several samples from around the garden, and test each one separately.

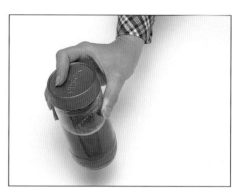

2 Use a measure such as the lid of an aerosol can, and mix 1 part soil to 5 parts water. Shake or stir the soil and water in a clean jar, then allow it to settle – it may take anything between half an hour and a day to become reasonably clear (clay soils are the slowest).

3 Carefully draw off some clear liquid from the top few centimetres for the test.

4 Using the pipette, transfer the solution to the test and reference chambers of the plastic container.

5 Pour the powder from the capsule provided into the test chamber. Replace the cap and shake vigorously until the powder has been dispersed.

6 Wait for a few minutes for the colour to develop, then read it off against the comparison chart. There will be a key that explains the implication of each reading, and accompanying instructions will tell you how to correct any problem.

APPLYING LIME

1 Try not to handle lime unnecessarily – ground limestone is relatively easy and safe to handle, but hydrated lime (the form often used) is slightly caustic. Use gloves and goggles when applying it. Divide the area into 1m (1yd) squares and weigh out enough for each square (see Box for rates), then if possible apply it with a spade, sprinkling it as evenly as possible.

2 Use a rake to cover the lime and work it into the ground.

HOW MUCH LIME?

Use the following table as a guide to the amount of lime needed to raise the pH of your soil by 1 pH. It is better to make several smaller applications over time than one big dose if you need to raise the pH by much. Test the soil again after a month, and apply more lime if necessary.

Do not apply lime at the same time as manure as there may be reaction that releases nitrogen in a form that can harm nearby plants, and it is wasteful of a useful fertilizer. Try to separate applications by several months.

TYPE OF SOIL	HYDRATED LIME	GROUND LIMESTONE
CLAY	640g/sq m (18oz/sq yd)	850g/sq m (24oz/sq yd)
AVERAGE LOAM	410g/sq m (12oz/sq yd)	550g/sq m (16oz/sq yd)
SAND	200g/sq m (6oz/sq yd)	275g/sq m (8oz/sq yd)

There are chemicals that will make the soil more acid, but this is seldom a very satisfactory solution. For the ornamental garden it is best to grow plants that like the soil you already have; for vegetables the best way to make a soil more acid is to add garden compost at the rate of 9kg/sq m (20lb/sq yd) or manure at the rate of 3kg/sq m (6lb/sq yd) to raise the acidity by about 1 pH.

A HANDY TEST

If you are not sure whether your soil is sandy, a medium loam, or clay, try the following test:

▪ Pick up a handful of damp but not wet soil and try to rub it between finger and thumb. If it feels gritty but the grains do not stick together, and it is difficult to roll into a ball, it is **sandy**.
▪ If it is gritty but can be rolled into a ball, it is a **sandy loam**.
▪ If it is gritty or sticky and can be rolled into a cylinder, it is **sandy clay loam** or a **clay loam**.
▪ If you can bend the cylinder into a ring, it is **clay**.

PROBE METER

Meters are even quicker to use than indicator kits, but some people think they are less accurate. It is important to use them carefully as recommended. Keep the probe clean and, if recommended by the manufacturer, keep the tip clean with very fine emery paper.

Push the probe into the soil and after a few moments read the pH shown on the dial. Make several attempts in the same area of ground to make sure that you get a consistent reading.

TESTING THE pH

The pH test is slightly different as you don't have to wait for the mixture to settle after the soil and water have been shaken together, and only the test chamber is filled with this solution. Fill the reference chamber with clean tap water.

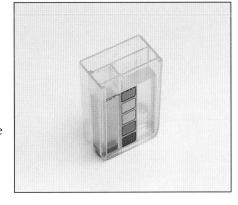

IMPROVING YOUR SOIL

Vegetables are good indicators of the condition of your soil. If they look vigorous and healthy you probably have nothing to worry about.

All soils benefit if you can add plenty of humus-forming material such as garden compost or well-rotted manure. Clay soils can also be improved by good drainage.

CREATING A SUMP

It may be possible to drain the land into a natural drain or ditch (check whether this is permissible first), otherwise make a sump in a low part of the garden and arrange the drains so that the water flows into it. The soakaway must be at least 60cm (2ft) deep. Fill it with rubble or gravel, top with inverted turves and cover with a layer of soil.

LAYING LAND DRAINS

1 Dig the trench for the drains at least 30cm (1ft) deep and with a slight fall. Place a layer of coarse grit or fine gravel along the bottom.

2 Traditional clay drains are still used, but you may find plastic equivalents like these at your local builder's merchant. Both kinds are satisfactory. Lay the drains on the bed of gravel.

SOIL CONDITIONERS

1 Dig in plenty of garden compost, well-rotted manure, or any organic matter that will quickly rot down in the soil. Peat and sharp sand will not rot down, but they help to improve the structure of the soil and aid drainage (sharp sand) or moisture-retention (peat or peat substitute).

2 If you can't easily dig more material into the soil because the area has already been planted, use plenty of organic mulches, such as garden compost or chipped bark, which will eventually be worked into the soil.

3 A heavy clay soil can be improved by applying lime (but only if this does not make it too alkaline for the plants you want to grow) and digging in a generous amount of *coarse* sand or grit. Also add plenty of compost or well-rotted manure. Concentrate on improving just a small area, rather than spreading the materials too thinly over a large area.

3 For side drains, use a T-shaped connector designed for the job. To ensure a close fit when using clay drains, score and cut the side drain with a cold chisel. Strike with firm blows to ensure a clean cut.

4 Pack coarse grit or fine gravel around the drains to improve drainage further and to reduce the chance of the pipes becoming clogged.

MAKING GARDEN COMPOST

It's almost impossible to have too much garden compost, so make as much as you can. You can form a compost heap without a container, but if you want to keep your compost looking tidy it's best to buy a bin or compost maker, or build one from scrap wood.

CONSTRUCTING A WOODEN BIN

1 The simplest way to build a wooden compost bin is to buy a kit. The wood will be pre-cut and ready to assemble. Most kits are assembled by slotting the pieces of wood together, or nailing the slats to the corner pieces provided.

2 The kit shown here is quick and easy to make. The pieces are hammered into the slots to form a sturdy bin. Once it has filled with compost, simply lift the entire bin away and start a new compost heap.

READY-MADE COMPOST BINS

A proprietary compost bin with lid.

This bin is suitable for compost or leaves.

MAKING COMPOST

1 To provide good aeration, place twiggy material at the bottom of the heap, then pile on kitchen and garden refuse that will rot down easily. Do not put on thick prunings unless they have been finely shredded first.

2 After adding 15cm (6in) of kitchen or garden refuse, add a layer of manure if possible. This will help to speed up the rotting process.

3 If manure is not available, sprinkle a thin layer of soil over every 15cm (6in) of refuse, to introduce more bacteria into the heap.

4 A proprietary compost activator will help to speed up the rotting process by stimulating the bacterial growth. You should not need to use an activator if the heap has had manure added to it.

TIPS FOR QUICK COMPOST

■ Use a bin or heap as large as possible – this generates more heat and increases the chance of the material rotting down more quickly.

■ Keep the material moist – be prepared to water it in dry weather if necessary.

■ Cover the top in wet weather if necessary to prevent waterlogging.

■ If possible, let in plenty of air at the base or sides.

■ In winter, cover the whole heap with an old carpet or something similar, to keep it warm and prevent waterlogging. Compost can take a long time to mature in cold weather.

■ To speed up the rotting process, fork out the compost after a few weeks, then fork it back into the bin, putting the old material from the outside towards the middle.

FERTILIZERS AND MANURES 1

Most gardeners happily use a combination of organic and inorganic fertilizers, but some prefer the organic-only approach. The important point to remember is that feeding will make a difference, especially to vegetables, seedlings and plants grown in containers. The benefit to shrubs and trees is usually less obvious, and it is best only to feed these in response to a known deficiency.

APPLYING FERTILIZERS

1 Apply fertilizers as evenly as possible. Divide unplanted ground into strips 90cm (3ft) wide, and work along these in 90cm (3ft) 'bites', scattering the appropriate amount of fertilizer for the area. Alternatively use a wheeled fertilizer spreader.

2 Rake it in when the area is complete. This will help to distribute the fertilizer more evenly as well as work it into the soil.

3 Vegetables sometimes need a boost during growth. Scatter the fertilizer along either side of the row, keeping it off the leaves. Hoe it in afterwards.

4 Scatter the fertilizer in a circle around established shrubs and other large plants. This will concentrate it where the active feeding roots are, with less chance of feeding weeds. Do not apply the fertilizer beyond the spread of the plant, and keep it away from the stem.

5 Hoe the fertilizer in, so that it penetrates more rapidly. Unless rain is forecast soon, water it in thoroughly so that it is available to the plants more quickly.

GARDENING BASICS

INORGANIC FERTILIZERS

Ammonium sulphate (sulphate of ammonia) supplies nitrogen, but makes the soil more acid.

Nitro-chalk supplies nitrogen without making the soil more acid.

Potassium sulphate (sulphate of potash) supplies potassium.

Superphosphate of lime (sometimes shortened to 'superphosphate') supplies phosphorus. Triple superphosphate is similar but almost three times stronger, so make sure that you apply the right kind of superphosphate of lime at an appropriate rate.

Balanced fertilizers (such as Growmore in the UK – which is a formulation, not a trade name) contain all the main nutrients: nitrogen, phosphorus and potassium.

Compound fertilizers are usually the same as balanced fertilizers, but do not always contain all three major nutrients.

Controlled- and slow-release fertilizers contain the major nutrients in a form that is released slowly over a period of months. In the case of controlled-release fertilizers, this is regulated by the temperature of the soil.

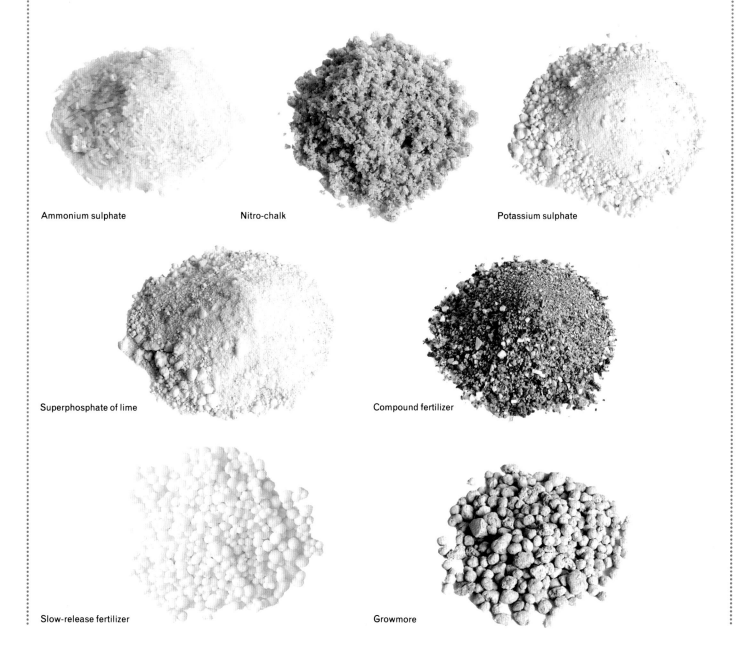

Ammonium sulphate

Nitro-chalk

Potassium sulphate

Superphosphate of lime

Compound fertilizer

Slow-release fertilizer

Growmore

Fertilizers And Manures 2

Organic gardeners prefer to use fertilizers that occur as natural products. Most of them are useful even if you do not garden organically.

ORGANIC FERTILIZERS

Blood, fish and bonemeal contains all the major nutrients. The nitrogen content is released quickly.

Bonemeal is a popular slow-acting fertilizer containing mainly phosphorus but also some nitrogen. 'Steamed' bonemeal should be safe to handle – unsterilized bonemeal carries a very small risk of harbouring diseases.

Dried animal manures are available in various types. They usually contain only a trace of the major nutrients, but a full range of trace elements (those nutrients needed only in very small quantities).

Dried blood is a fast-acting nitrogenous fertilizer. Use it when the plants need a quick boost of growth during the summer.

Fish meal contains nitrogen and phosphorus.

Hoof and horn contains nitrogen in a form that is released slowly. It is a more suitable source of nitrogen than dried blood for sustained growth.

Liquid animal manures contain a small amount of all the major nutrients, plus a full range of trace elements.

Liquid seaweed contains a useful amount of nitrogen and potassium, but only a trace of phosphorus. It is good for supplying trace elements and some growth hormones.

Seaweed meal contains all the major nutrients, plus many minor ones and trace elements. It is a very good all-round fertilizer, but is best applied when the soil is warm so that the bacteria can break it down.

Wood ash – the exact chemical analysis will depend on the material burned, but there will be a useful amount of potassium and a small amount of phosphorus.

BULKY MANURES AND COMPOST

Garden compost, well-rotted animal manures, and bulky organic materials such as spent mushroom compost and spent hops usually add only small amounts of fertilizer. They are invaluable, however, because they help to improve the soil structure, its water-holding capacity, and even the ability of the soil to retain nutrients applied from other sources.

Dried chicken manure

Blood, fish and bonemeal

Bonemeal

Dried blood

GREEN MANURING

1 Green manuring is a way of adding humus to the soil without making a compost heap. First fork over the ground cleared of an earlier crop.

2 Scatter mustard seed (or any other type of seed sold for green manuring) so that it covers the ground quite thickly.

3 Rake over the soil to bury the mustard seed completely.

4 When the mustard is about 30cm (12in) high, and before it flowers and sets seed, dig it into the ground. It will eventually rot and release both humus and nutrients for a later crop.

Fish meal

Liquid seaweed

Seaweed meal

Hoof and horn

WATERING

Watering by hand is a chore that most gardeners prefer to avoid, but there are ways to make the job easier, and automatic watering systems will eliminate the hard work and be better for the plants.

DRIP FEEDS

1 A system like this one will solve most of your watering problems. You can run both spray and drip nozzles off the same system. Connect the master unit to a hose from the mains. The master unit reduces the water pressure and contains a filter that can be removed for cleaning.

2 Run the main supply tube where it will not be too visible, such as beneath a hedge, or submerged just beneath the soil.

3 Connect the smaller-diameter branch tubes with the special connectors wherever you need to take water to a particular part of the garden.

4 Use drip-feed heads to water containers and individual plants in a border. The special pegs provided will enable you to hold the tube in a suitable position.

5 Use a spray head for more general watering, such as for flower beds or rows of vegetables. This particular system offers a range of nozzles to provide different water droplet sizes and areas covered.

CHOOSING AN APPROPRIATE SPRINKLER

Oscillating sprinklers are useful for rectangular lawns and seed beds. They can usually be adjusted to cover areas of different sizes.
Static sprinklers are intended mainly for lawns, but they generally water in a circular pattern, so you will have to keep moving them around to achieve even coverage. They are mostly inexpensive.

Rotating sprinklers water in a circular pattern. The droplets are thrown out by rotating arms driven by the water pressure. They usually cover a wider area than static sprinklers.

If you want to water a flower bed or vegetable plot, buy a version with a head on a long spike. The head must be clear of surrounding foliage.

Pulse-jet sprinklers have a single jet on a central pivot that rotates in a series of pulses, each time ejecting a spurt of water. These water in a circular pattern, but are efficient and can cover a very wide area. Those intended for lawns usually have a low base, but if the water needs to be thrown clear of surrounding foliage, buy one on a long stem.

Oscillating sprinkler

Static sprinkler

Rotating sprinkler

Pulse-jet sprinkler

TAPS AND TIMERS

An outdoor tap is invaluable, and essential if you have a drip-feed watering system. Outdoor tap kits are readily available, and these contain all the parts and instructions for fitting.

In the UK you must fit a non-return valve. These are widely available, and some outdoor taps already have them fitted.

If you have installed an automatic watering system, go one step further and install a tap computer that will turn the water supply on and off at programmed times, even when you are not there.

SEEP HOSES

Seep hoses are designed to be laid along the ground for long-term watering. The tiny perforations deliver the water slowly so that it seeps well down into the soil. You can use seep hoses in flower beds or borders, but they are especially useful for irrigating rows of fruit or vegetables.

SEEPAGE HOSE

Some seepage hoses are made of a porous rubber. The water seeps slowly from the surface. Lay a seepage hose on top of the soil like an ordinary seep hose, or bury it in a shallow slit trench 10–15cm (4–6in) deep. You may find this visually more acceptable in a shrub or herbaceous border.

WEEDING BEDS AND BORDERS

Weeds not only look unsightly but they also affect the growth of your plants by competing for water and nutrients. To win the battle against weeds, you need a plan of campaign and to carry it through with determination. Once you are in control, weeding should be no more than a minor occasional chore.

HAND-WEEDING

1 Some hand-weeding will always be necessary, but forking out deep-rooted perennials such as nettles and dandelions should be required only when you clear the ground. Later, seedlings should never be allowed to become so well established. Use a fork to loosen the roots, and hold the main stem close to the soil so that you can pull up the whole root system. If the root won't lift without tearing, dig deeper.

2 Even difficult perennial weeds are easy to control if you remove them while they are still young. Make sure that you remove the whole root, but a hand fork should be adequate for lifting the plant.

3 Regular hoeing will keep most weeds under control. Hoe in dry weather, and slice the weeds off below the surface, holding the hoe so that the blade is parallel to the soil's surface. This is a Dutch hoe, useful for weeding along straight rows, but there are other designs and proprietary hoes that you might find more useful for specific situations.

4 A hand cultivator with prongs which may be removed can be useful for loosening the soil and weeds along rows of vegetables. However, it is not as efficient as a hoe when slicing off weeds.

CHEMICAL WEEDING

1 Use a chemical weedkiller if you want to clear the ground of weeds quickly. Some weedkillers will just kill the top growth, so are best for annual weeds, while others will kill the roots too. Others will inhibit the growth of new seedlings. Be sure to choose one appropriate to your needs.

Spray drift from a weedkiller is a real hazard to your plants. Always choose a calm day for spraying and fit a dribble bar to the watering can. Hold the bar close to the ground. Keep a watering can exclusively for applying weedkillers and label it clearly.

2 Most weedkillers will begin to act within days, and after a week the weeds will show clear signs of dying. Some weed-killers are inactivated by contact with the soil, and you can sow or plant as soon as you have cleared away the dead growth. If you use a weedkiller that is translocated to the roots to kill difficult perennial weeds, wait until the top growth has died down before removing the weeds – this gives the weedkiller time to work properly.

3 If you have difficult, deep-rooted perennial weeds growing among desirable plants, making spraying impossible, paint a translocated weedkiller (such as one based on glyphosate) on to individual weeds.

MULCH CONTROL

2 Where appearance matters, such as in a flower or shrub border, cover any bare ground with a 5cm (2in) layer of chipped bark or other decorative mulch.

1 Black polythene sheeting controls weeds very effectively. Where appearance does not matter, lay it along the rows. Tuck the edges in a shallow trench and cover with soil, or just weight down with bricks. Alternatively, hold in place with proprietary pegs sold for the purpose.

Weeding Lawns And Paths

When hand-weeding was the only option, a weed-free lawn or path was either a dream or exceptionally hard work. Nowadays selective weedkillers, which attack most of the weeds but not the grass, enable anyone to achieve a super lawn . . . and long-lasting path weedkillers mean clear paths all year round with just one or two applications.

Lawn Weedkillers

1 Most selective lawn weedkillers are diluted and applied as a liquid. To be sure of covering the area evenly, use two lengths of string to mark out the width of the dribble bar used with your watering can.

2 At the end of each row, move one of the strings across to mark out the next strip. Always follow the manufacturer's suggested rate of application.

3 If your lawn also needs feeding, save time with a weed-and-feed for lawns. This contains a combined fertilizer and weedkiller, but use it only when the lawn needs weeding, and follow the manufacturer's advice. There are different mixtures for spring, summer and autumn use. Apply with a fertilizer spreader if you want to save even more time.

4 It is wasteful to apply a selective weedkiller to the whole lawn if you have just a few weeds in small patches. You can apply a liquid weedkiller to small patches of lawn, but a wipe-on stick containing a selective weedkiller is a quick, cheap and easy method of dealing with just a few isolated weeds.

HAND-WEEDING A LAWN

1 Weeding trowels are useful for prising up weeds such as dandelions and daisies. Push the tool in just behind the root and lift the plant with a lever action as you pull with the other hand. Even deep-rooted plants can usually be removed like this.

2 Firm the soil again afterwards to make it less suitable for weed seedlings to germinate. If you have had to lift a lot of weeds that were close together, there may be a bare patch. It is worth sprinkling a few grass seeds over the patch rather than leaving bare soil for more weed seedlings to grow.

DEALING WITH COARSE GRASS

If you have a small clump of very coarse grass growing in your lawn, either dig it up and reseed the area, or keep slashing through it with a knife. This will eventually weaken it and allow the finer grasses to grow over the area.

PATH WEEDKILLERS

1 Path weedkillers will kill all plants that they touch, and most will remain active in the soil for many months. Always choose a still day to reduce the risk of wind blowing the spray around the garden. A watering can with a dribble bar will apply larger drops than most sprayers and these are less likely to blow around.

2 Shield plants with a sheet of cardboard, plywood or plastic if you are applying a weedkiller to a path near a border.

PEST CONTROL 1: APHIDS AND OTHER SAP-SUCKERS

Sap-sucking insects are particularly unpleasant pests because they transmit virus diseases by injecting infected sap from one plant into another. They also cause distorted growth if they attack developing buds, and generally weaken the plants that they feed on. Always deal with aphids promptly.

IDENTIFICATION

Aphids are among the best-known insect pests. Greenfly and blackfly are the common ones, but there are many species, some affecting the roots of plants rather than the

CHEMICAL CONTROL

Many leaf-sucking insects hide on the undersides of leaves. Always make sure that you cover the undersides of the leaves as well as the tops – especially if using a contact insecticide.

leaves. Foliage may be sticky from the honeydew excreted by the aphids – with a black mould.
Control with any contact insecticide recommended for aphids. Systemic insecticide is likely to be more effective on ornamental plants.
Green controls include insecticidal soaps and pirimicarb.
Leaf hoppers are usually green or yellow insects 2–3mm (1/16–1/8in) long. They leap when disturbed.
Control with most contact and systemic insecticides.
Red spider mites are tiny creatures about 2mm (1/16in) long. You are more likely to notice their fine, silky webs and a pale mottling on the upper surface of leaves rather than the pests themselves.
Control with a contact insecticide, or a systemic insecticide.
Green control is best achieved with the predatory mite *Phytoseiulus persimilis* and high humidity.
Scale insects are immobile and scale-like in appearance, usually yellow, brown, dark grey or white, and up to 6mm (1/4in) long.
Control with a contact insecticide recommended for scale.

Thrips are narrow brownish-black insects up to 2mm (1/16in) long. Affected leaves have a silvery-white discoloration on the upper surface.
Control with a systemic insecticide.
Green control is best with a 'natural' relatively harmless insecticide such as one based on pyrethrum. Be prepared to spray frequently.
Whitefly look like tiny white moths, and often rise up in a cloud when disturbed. The wingless nymphs are whitish-green and scale-like.
Control with any of the contact insecticides recommended for whitefly, but be prepared to repeat the treatment frequently.
Green control is with a parasitic wasp, *Encarsia formosa*, but this is suitable only for the greenhouse.

BIOLOGICAL CONTROL

Biological controls are available for some sap-sucking pests. *Encarsia formosa* is a parasitic wasp that will help to control whitefly. Hang the pack on the plants that you want to protect. The parasites will emerge and in time will start to breed.

Blackfly Whitefly Symptoms of red spider mite Leaf hopper damage Scale

PEST CONTROL 2: LEAF-EATERS

Leaf-eating pests can soon devastate a plant. If the culprits are caterpillars you will easily identify the cause, but many leaf-eaters move on, so tracking them down may call for a little deduction.

IDENTIFICATION

Caterpillars come in many shapes and sizes, but you will certainly recognize them even if you don't

CHEMICAL CONTROL

Slug pellets are very effective at controlling slugs and snails. Most are coloured blue to make them unattractive to birds. If you are worried about pets eating the pellets, place them in pieces of narrow drainpipe or something similar.

It is unnecessary to space them more closely than is recommended by the manufacturer – about 15cm (6in) apart is close enough.

know the species. You will find them on the affected leaves.

Control with derris dust or another contact insecticide recommended for caterpillars.

Green controls include picking off by hand and spraying with the bacterial control *Bacillus thuringiensis*.

Earwigs are yellowish-brown insects about 12mm (½in) long, with curved pincers at the rear.

Control with insecticidal powders for crawling insects, dusted around the base of the plant, or sprayed on at dusk, which are more effective than normal contact sprays.

Green control is to make a trap of a pot stuffed with straw, placed on top of a cane. The earwigs will shelter in this during the day. Empty the pot periodically and destroy the insects.

Slugs and snails are too well-known to need description. Symptoms range from holes in the leaves to foliage that is completely eaten, or stripped down to the main stalks. The pest may have moved on or gone into hiding, but slime trails are often a give-away.

Control with slug pellets.

Green control involves making or buying beer traps so that the pests drown in a state of intoxication. Protect vulnerable plants in the spring by sprinkling coarse grit around crowns and new shoots.

Weevils eat irregularly-shaped holes around the edges of leaves. The mature insects are usually grey or black with a short snout and elbowed antennae.

Control by spraying with an insecticide recommended for the pest, preferably at dusk.

Green control by biological control is being developed.

BIOLOGICAL CONTROL

Many kinds of caterpillar can be controlled with a bacterium that causes a disease in the insects. If you spray the food plants of the pest species (such as cabbages) you should not upset the health of the population of decorative butterflies that feed on weeds.

Mix up the spray as recommended by the manufacturer, and spray before the caterpillars have become a major problem.

Caterpillar damage

Snail damage

Earwig damage

Slug damage

Weevils

PEST CONTROL 3: ROOT-EATERS

Root pests often go unnoticed until the plants collapse, but many of them can be controlled successfully if you are vigilant.

IDENTIFICATION
Cutworms and leatherjackets
Cutworms are the caterpillars of various moths, and have a typical caterpillar shape. They are usually brown and live in the soil, though they may feed above soil level at night. The base of the stem is usually gnawed, and the plant slowly wilts and will probably die. Leatherjackets are the larvae of daddy-long-legs, or crane flies, and have tubular grey bodies about 2.5–4cm (1–1½in) long.
Control by treating the affected plants with a soil insecticide as soon as you notice the damage.
Green control consists of winter digging where applicable, to expose the grubs to birds, and picking the pests off by hand whenever you find them.

Root flies are numerous, and affect vegetables such as carrots and onions, but also bulbs. There are many different species, and it is the larvae that do the damage by eating the roots.
Control is difficult or impossible once the grubs are in the roots. Where these pests are known to be a problem, use a soil insecticide when planting or sowing.
Green control consists of always firming the soil around the roots when planting or thinning, and not leaving thinnings on the surface (the smell may attract the flies). Carrot fly can be deterred by erecting a polythene barrier about 45cm (18in) tall around the plants. This works because the pests only fly close to the ground.

BIOLOGICAL CONTROL

Carrot flies keep close to the ground, so a low physical barrier like a fine net mesh may be enough to prevent them laying their eggs around the plants.

Weevils There are several species, and it is the grubs that damage plant roots. If a small plant collapses and you find small curved white grubs with brown heads and no legs on the remains of the roots, these are likely to be weevil grubs.
Control is difficult, and soil insecticides have only a limited degree of success.
Green control is possible with a nematode, which affects the grubs, but this solution is only just becoming widely available at the time of writing.

CHEMICAL CONTROL

Ordinary insecticides are not very effective in the soil. Use a product recommended for soil pests. Some are available as powders to sprinkle on affected areas, others are sprays to be applied to the soil.

Root fly larvae

Root fly damage

Grubs of weevils

Disease Control 1: Leaf Diseases

Fungus diseases affect the leaves of many plants, and often they are difficult to control. Where possible grow varieties that have a disease resistance, and always spray or remove affected leaves at the first sign of trouble.

IDENTIFICATION

Downy mildew looks like a fluffy or mealy white growth on the surface of the leaf. This may be most obvious on the underside, with just brown or yellow blotches on the top surface.

Control by removing the affected leaves, then spraying the plant with a fungicide recommended for this disease. Sprays that control powdery mildew may not be very effective against downy mildew.

Green control consists of picking off affected leaves as soon as the disease is noticed. Make sure that the plants have good ventilation and are not overcrowded.

Leaf spots affect many plants, and rose black spot is just one kind. The spots or blotches are usually black, brown or yellow.

Control is best achieved by a systemic fungicide (except for edible crops).

Green control is difficult, but good garden hygiene (destroying affected leaves promptly) will limit the spread of these diseases.

Powdery mildew looks like a white powdery deposit on the leaves, and is most commonly found on the upper surface.

Downy mildew

Leaf spot

Powdery mildew

Rust

Control and green control are as for downy mildew, except that you have a wider choice of chemicals.

Rusts vary in appearance depending on the type, but most cause yellowish patches on the upper surface of the leaves and corresponding small brown or orange patches on the reverse sides of the leaves.

Control with one of the few fungicides that control rust reasonably well (check the label to see if the product is recommended for rust – many fungicides are not effective). Remove affected leaves to prevent the disease spreading.

Green control is best achieved by picking off and destroying all affected leaves as soon as they are noticed, and ensuring adequate spacing and ventilation.

BIOLOGICAL CONTROL

You can achieve a lot simply by picking off diseased leaves as soon as they are noticed, to prevent the problem spreading. Always collect dead leaves at the end of the season, but do not use diseased leaves for compost.

CHEMICAL CONTROL

Roses and other plants prone to fungus diseases are best sprayed on a regular basis with a systemic fungicide to keep them healthy and disease-free.

Disease Control 2: Root Diseases

Most root diseases are a minor inconvenience that crops up from time to time, but club-root is a serious problem that will restrict the types of plants that you can grow successfully.

Identification

Blackleg affects cuttings. The base turns black, shrinks and becomes soft. The cutting eventually dies.
Control is impossible once blackleg occurs, but using a rooting hormone that contains a fungicide may prevent it happening.
Green control is not practical – just remove and destroy affected cuttings promptly.
Club-root affects members of the *Cruciferae* family, especially brassicas such as cabbages and swedes and a few ornamentals such as wallflowers. The roots become swollen and distorted, and growth is very stunted.
Control of club-root is difficult because the disease remains in the soil for many years. Use a proprietary club-root dip before planting out the seedlings.
Green control is best achieved by growing the seedlings in pots of sterilized compost – they will get off to a good start and be better able to resist the worst effects of the disease. Keep down weeds that are a potential source of infection.
Foot and root rots affect a number of plants such as peas, beans, tomatoes, cucumbers and even bedding plants such as petunias. The roots turn black and the base of the stem starts to rot.
Control with chemicals is not practical for foot and root rots.
Green control is the most effective: try to avoid growing the same plants in the same ground each year, raise plants in sterilized compost and destroy affected plants as soon as they are noticed.
Storage rots affect bulbs and corms in storage, as well as stored onions. Soft patches appear, and sometimes the surface area is covered with fungal growth.
Control by dusting non-edible bulbs, tubers and corms with a fungicide before storing.
Green control is effective. Always make sure that the bulbs are dry before storing them, and keep in a cool but frost-free, airy place. Check every few weeks and remove any soft bulbs before they can affect the others.

Chemical Control

Non-edible bulbs, corms and tubers will be less likely to rot in store if you first treat them with a fungicide. Dust them with a suitable powder, or use a fungicidal dip (be sure to dry them off thoroughly afterwards).

Biological Control

Bulbs, corms and tubers will be less likely to rot if you hang them up in something where air can circulate freely, like a net or even a pair of old tights or stockings.

Blackleg

PHYSIOLOGICAL AND OTHER PROBLEMS

Some problems that at first appear to be caused by pests or diseases have physiological causes (like wind chill or sun scorch). Others are caused by accidents with weedkillers, or even by nutritional deficiencies in the soil.

IDENTIFICATION

Cold damage is most likely to occur on evergreens that are not completely hardy. The leaves are blackened or brown, and often puckered or withered. Prune out affected parts – many plants will soon outgrow limited damage.

Fasciated stems can be caused by many factors, such as injury or a genetic quirk. The stems are flattened and may look as though two stems are fused together. No harm is caused to the plant.

Iron and manganese deficiencies are most likely on chalky soils. Both create similar symptoms: yellowing leaves, especially at the edges or between the veins. If caused by a soil with a high pH, apply sequestered iron or trace elements in a chelated or fritted formulation.

Nitrogen deficiency shows itself in pale green leaves, sometimes mottled or flushed yellow. Growth is usually slow. Feed with a high-nitrogen fertilizer.

Potassium deficiency shows itself in leaves that look prematurely autumnal, with a yellow or purplish flush or blotches, and brown margins. The leaves sometimes roll inwards. Apply a sulphate of potash or some other fertilizer high in potassium.

Sun scorch happens behind unshaded glass in a greenhouse or where the temperature is exceptionally high. Brown patches on the upper exposed surface of the leaf are early signs, but the edges of the leaves may also turn brown and brittle. Solve the problem by providing better shading for the plant during hot, sunny weather and plenty of ventilation.

Weedkiller damage depends on the type of weedkiller involved. Selective hormone weedkillers used in lawns will cause distorted growth if they drift on to nearby ornamental plants. Contact weedkillers usually cause pale or bleached areas on the foliage, which may turn almost white. Eventually it turns brown and black. There is nothing you can do, except to be more careful when applying another time.

Viruses come in many forms, causing different symptoms. Usually the leaves have a mottled pattern, or a yellowish mosaic effect, or yellow stripes, and the plant is generally stunted. Not all viruses are regarded as undesirable – some striped flowers and variegated leaves which are caused by virus infections are regarded as attractive. Generally, however, all plants that have been affected by a virus should be pulled up and destroyed as soon as possible.

Cold damage

Manganese deficiency

Iron deficiency

Fasciated stem

Nitrogen deficiency

Sun scorch

Virus infection

SOWING IN POTS AND TRAYS

Tender bedding plants must be started off indoors or in the greenhouse. Sow in trays if you need a lot of plants, but if you need just a few, sow in pots to save space. Many hardy plants such as rock plants and hardy border perennials can be sown in pots and trays, but to save space indoors you can put them out in a cold frame to germinate.

SOWING IN POTS

1 For border perennials, rock plants, house plants and shrubs, where you will not need many plants, sow in pots to save space. Make yourself a rounded presser to firm down the compost, or improvise with a jam-jar or something similar.

2 Sprinkle the seeds over the compost as evenly as possible, using the sand technique described below if the seed is very fine. Stand the pot in a bowl of water and let it seep through to moisten the compost. Remove it and let it drain.

3 Insert a label then cover with a sheet of glass or put the pot into a propagator if the seeds need warmth for germination.

4 Some seeds, particularly alpines and shrubs, do not need much warmth and are often better in cool conditions initially. Place these in a cold frame instead of a propagator. Plunging the pots in sand reduces the risk of the compost drying out.

SOWING FINE SEED

1 If the seed is very fine and difficult to handle, mix it with a small quantity of silver sand to make even distribution easier.

2 Sprinkle the sand and seed mix as evenly as possible between your finger and thumb, as if sprinkling salt over food. Very fine seed will need only a very shallow covering or no covering at all.

1 Fill the tray loosely with a sterilized compost suitable for seeds (do not use a potting compost). Strike off the compost so it is level with the rim, then press it down with a piece of wood that will fit inside the tray. Leave the compost about 12mm (½in) below the rim. Water the tray with a fine-rosed can *before* sowing. If you water afterwards you might wash the seeds away or cause them to drift to one side of the tray.

2 Sprinkle the seeds as thinly as possible over the surface. Large seeds can be spaced individually. To space medium-sized seeds fold over a piece of stiff paper to hold the seeds, then tap it with a finger as you move it over the surface.

3 Cover the seeds by sifting more compost over the top. Always check the seed packet to find whether or not the seeds should be covered. Some seeds germinate better if exposed to light.

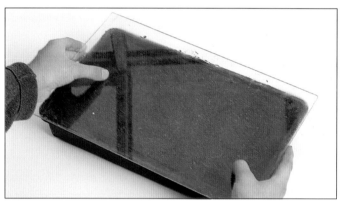

4 Cover the tray with a sheet of glass to prevent the compost drying out. If you don't have a sheet of glass, place the tray in a polythene bag. Tuck the end under or seal it with a plastic-covered wire twist-tie. Don't forget to label the tray.

5 Turn the glass over, or the bag inside out, daily to prevent condensation drips becoming a problem.

6 You should remove the glass or plastic bag as soon as the seeds begin to germinate. If you leave them covered for too long, the humid environment created may encourage the growth of fungal diseases that can kill the seedlings.

PRICKING OUT

As soon as seedlings are large enough to handle, prick them out into pots or trays of potting compost so they have the space and nutrients necessary for healthy growth.

PRICKING OUT INTO TRAYS

1 Fill the tray with a sterilized potting compost. Strike it level and firm to leave the compost about 12mm (½in) below the rim.

2 Use a small dibber or a tool designed for pricking out seedlings to loosen the compost and lift out each seedling with as much compost as possible attached.

3 Use the small dibber or planting tool to make a hole deep enough to take the roots, and transplant the seedling while holding it by one of its seed leaves (the first leaves to open). Firm the compost gently around the roots. Space the seedlings about 2.5–5cm (1–2in) apart, depending on the needs of the plant.

4 Water the plants thoroughly after transplanting, using a watering can with a fine rose. Shade from direct sunlight for a couple of days.

PRICKING OUT INTO MODULES

Pricking out into modules, or trays with pre-formed compartments, will ensure even spacing and cause less root damage when you transplant the seedlings.

Transplanting Into Pots

1 Pot plants such as cyclamen, greenhouse plants like tomatoes and cucumbers, and large bedding plants such as dahlias are best pricked out into individual pots instead of trays. The seedlings have more space to grow and more compost to sustain them. Loosen the plants as described for pricking out into trays, but place them in small 8–10cm (3–4in) pots.

2 After watering, keep the pots out of direct sunlight for a couple of days. Square pots are more space-saving than round pots for the same volume of compost.

Plugs And Pot-ready Plants

1 Seedlings are sometimes sold in 'plugs' (small individual blocks of compost). You can also grow your own seedlings like this, using the small plastic trays designed for the purpose (sow one or two seeds in each cell, and thin to one plant if necessary).

2 Transplant the seedlings into seed trays or pots, spacing them as you would seedlings sown in a tray. Young plants are sometimes sold by nurseries and garden centres in larger plugs of compost, or in special small peat containers. These larger plants are best potted up individually rather than grown in trays.

Sowing in 'cells' or modules saves the tricky and time-consuming job of pricking out. Just sow a couple of seeds in each cell then pull out any surplus if more than one germinates. The technique is suitable for most bedding plants and many vegetables that are started off in the greenhouse.

SOWING HARDY ANNUALS

Hardy annuals are undemanding plants that you can sow directly into the garden, where the plants are to flower. Provided you thin them out and water in dry weather while they are small, you will have masses of colourful flowers for the minimum of effort.

SOWING IN ROWS

1 Make sure that the area is free of weeds, then rake the ground level. Break down any large lumps of earth so that the seeds have fine soil in which to germinate.

2 For a bright bed of annuals, mark out the areas in which each kind is to grow, using sand or grit to indicate the boundary of each drift of colour.

3 Take out shallow drills with a hoe or the corner of a rake, at a spacing appropriate to the type of plant. Alternate the direction of the drills in each marked area, as this will make the bed look less strictly regimented.

4 Sow the seeds as evenly as possible. Space large or pelleted seeds individually, otherwise take a few seeds at a time and scatter them as evenly as possible along the drill.

5 Label each section, then rake the soil level to cover the seeds.

6 Water whenever the weather is dry until all the seedlings have germinated and are well established.

Hardy annuals are the easiest of all flowers to grow. They can be sown where they are to flower, usually bloom quickly, and in the majority of cases are bright and cheerful. These are godetias.

SOWING BROADCAST

1 Packets of mixed annuals and groups of one type that are to be grown in a less formal way can be sown broadcast (scattered randomly). At the seedling stage, however, it is more difficult to tell which are annuals and which are weed seedlings, but this is a quicker way to sow. Just scatter the seeds over the area as evenly as possible.

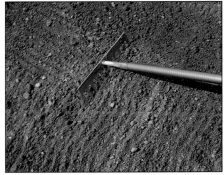

2 Rake the seeds in to distribute and bury them. Rake first in one direction and then at right angles.

THINNING

Thin the seedlings while still young to prevent overcrowding. Hold the soil down on either side of the plant you want to retain while pulling out the unwanted plants. Leave the seedlings spaced at the distances recommended on the packet. Water after thinning if the weather is dry.

Sowing Alpines And Shrubs

Alpine and tree and shrub seeds often need to undergo a period of cold weather, and many germinate better if you sow them in the autumn and overwinter them in a cold frame.

Sowing Slow-germinating Perennials

1 Fill a small pot with a loam-based seed compost and firm it gently to provide a flat surface for sowing.

2 Sow the seed fairly thickly as germination is often poor or erratic, but do not let the seeds touch one another.

3 Cover the seeds with more potting compost, then sprinkle grit or coarse sand over the surface to discourage the growth of algae and keep the surface well aerated.

4 Plunge the pots up to their rims in a cold frame to keep the compost moist. If the seeds are fleshy and attractive to mice, cover the pots with a sheet of glass.

Pricking Out

Don't forget to label the pots — especially if you have sown more than one kind of seed. And remember to keep the compost watered whenever necessary. Seedlings will usually start to germinate in the spring and during the summer. Prick them out and grow on in pots or in rows in a nursery bed (see opposite).

LEFT Aubretias are particularly easy alpines to raise from seed, and they flower quickly. Although they generally do not grow true to type from seed, they are often just as good as named varieties from cuttings.

BIENNIALS AND PERENNIALS

1 An easy way to grow biennials and border perennials is to sow the seeds in a seed bed in the garden in late spring or early summer. Choose a vacant piece of ground for sowing, making sure that it is neither too dry nor too shaded.

2 Take out shallow drills in rows about 23cm (9in) apart, and sow the seeds thinly. Water the rows gently, then rake the soil over the seeds.

3 If you have sown too thickly, thin some of the seedlings. When the seedlings are 5–8cm (2–3in) high, prepare another piece of ground where the plants can grow on until the autumn. Rake in a general garden fertilizer.

4 Space the seedlings 15–23cm (6–9in) apart to allow them enough space to grow during the summer. Water well.

5 Biennials such as wallflowers and sweet Williams will make better and bushier plants if you pinch out the growing tips a few weeks after transplanting. Lift biennials in the autumn, once summer bedding has been cleared, and plant them in their flowering positions. Leave border perennials until the following spring before moving to their final positions.

SOFTWOOD AND GREENWOOD CUTTINGS

Softwood and greenwood cuttings root quickly and easily, and you can take them from popular plants like pelargoniums (geraniums) and fuchsias. Greenwood cuttings are similar to softwood cuttings, but are taken from the soft tip of the stem after the first flush of early growth has slowed down.

KEEPING CUTTINGS FRESH

Softwood cuttings soon wilt, so put them in a polythene bag until you are ready to insert them into the compost.

TAKING SOFTWOOD CUTTINGS

1 Many shrubs, as well as pelargoniums (geraniums), can be propagated from the soft new shoots produced during the early flush of growth. The length of the cutting is not critical, but do cut below the third leaf or pair of leaves from the tip.

2 Trim off the lowest pair of leaves. If the plant has stipules (small scale-like growths at the base of each leaf stalk), as pelargoniums do, pull these off too. Trim the base of the stem with a sharp knife or blade, cutting straight across the stem just below a leaf joint.

3 Dip the cut tip of each cutting into a rooting powder containing a fungicide.

4 Use a dibber to make a hole in a pot of cuttings compost for the cutting.

5 Insert the cuttings around the edge of the pot, without overcrowding them. Alternatively, place each cutting in a small individual pot. After watering, place in a warm and humid propagator, or cover with a polythene bag, and keep in a warm light place out of direct sunlight. If a number of cuttings have been planted together in one pot, pot up individually once each plant has formed plenty of roots.

TAKING GREENWOOD CUTTINGS

1 Take the cuttings once the new growth has begun to slow down – usually in early summer. The length will depend on the plant, but for most shrubs remove the top 10cm (4in) of the shoot.

2 Put the cuttings into a polythene bag or a bowl of water until you are ready to prepare them, otherwise they will wilt rapidly.

3 Shorten the length of each cutting to about 8cm (3in), though you must adjust this to suit the plant. Cut straight across the stem just below a leaf joint.

4 Trim the leaves from the bottom half of the cutting, using a sharp knife.

5 Dip the cut ends into a rooting hormone, to ensure speedy rooting.

6 Insert the cuttings around the edge of a pot, then water with a fungicide and leave to drain.

7 Place the pot in a warm and humid propagator in a light place out of direct sunlight. If you don't have a propagator, cover the pot with a polythene bag instead.

BASAL STEM CUTTINGS

Basal stem cuttings can be taken in spring from many herbaceous plants that produce a cluster of new shoots from the soil level at this time. It's also a good method if you want to propagate more dahlias than division of the tubers would give you.

1 Use the basal shoots of delphiniums and lupins to make new plants. Remove the shoots when they are about 8–10cm (3–4in) long, cutting them off just above the surface.

2 Trim the cuttings cleanly with a sharp knife across the end, and remove any low leaves that would be below compost level when the cutting has been inserted. Dip the ends into a rooting hormone.

3 Insert the cuttings, one to a pot or two or three around the edge of a pot, and firm the compost gently. A mixture of peat and sand or a rooting compost should be used. Cover the cuttings to provide a humid atmosphere until they root.

Chrysanthemum

TAKING DAHLIA CUTTINGS

1 In late winter place the tubers in boxes or deep trays and pack moist compost or peat around them. Keep in a warm, light place.

2 When the shoots have grown to about 8cm (3in) long, cut them off close to the tuber.

3 Remove the lowest leaves from each cutting, and trim the cuttings straight just below a leaf joint with a sharp knife or razor blade.

4 Dip the cut ends into a rooting hormone, then insert several cuttings into each pot of rooting compost. Keep moist and pot up individually once they have rooted.

TAKING CHRYSANTHEMUM CUTTINGS

1 Whether the cuttings have been placed in boxes in the greenhouse or the plants have been overwintered outdoors, cut off young shoots about 3–5cm (1¼–2in) long. Pull off the lowest leaves and trim the end with a knife.

2 Insert the cuttings around the edge of a pot. They will usually root without a rooting hormone, but using one will improve the rate and speed of rooting.

3 Cover the pot with a polythene bag, inflated to ensure that it does not touch the cuttings. Check the cuttings regularly, turning the bag to avoid condensation dripping onto the leaves. Remove any leaves that start to rot.

Semi-ripe Cuttings

Semi-ripe (also called semi-mature) cuttings are an excellent way to propagate a wide range of shrubs. Mid and late summer are ideal times to take them, and most cuttings will have formed roots within a month or two – some will root after just a couple of weeks.

TAKING SEMI-RIPE CUTTINGS

1 Take cuttings from shoots that are more or less fully grown, except for the tips. The wood at the base should be beginning to harden even though the tip may still be soft. Make the cutting 5–10cm (2–4in) long, depending on the shrub.

2 Strip the lower leaves from each cutting, then trim it to a suitable length if necessary.

3 Use a rooting hormone, dipping just the cut end into the powder or liquid. If using a powder, dip the end of the cutting into water first, so the powder adheres more easily.

4 Semi-ripe cuttings taken during the summer will root in the open ground provided you keep them watered, but they will do better in a garden frame. Make a slit with a trowel or other tool, then insert the cuttings so they do not quite touch.

5 Firm the cuttings to make sure there are no large air pockets that would cause the cuttings or new roots to dry out.

6 Water the cuttings after planting, and keep an eye on them to make sure they do not dry out during the warm summer weather. It is worth adding a fungicide to the initial watering.

7 Label each row. By the time they root it is easy to forget what they are – especially if you take a lot of different summer cuttings.

Some Shrubs To Propagate

The following shrubs root easily from semi-ripe cuttings. But there are many others that will root successfully, so be prepared to experiment if your favourite shrub does not appear in the list.

Abelia
Buddleia (butterfly bush)
Camellia
Ceanothus (Californian lilac)
Chaenomeles (quince)
Choisya (Mexican orange blossom)
Cistus (sun rose)
Cotoneaster
Daphne
Deutzia
Elaeagnus
Escallonia
Euonymus
Forsythia
Fuchsia
Griselinia
Hebe
Helianthemum (rock rose)
Hibiscus
Hydrangea
Ligustrum (privet)
Philadelphus (mock orange)
Pieris
Potentilla
Pyracantha (firethorn)
Rhododendron
Ribes (flowering currant)
Rose
Rosemary
Santolina (cotton lavender)
Syringa (lilac)
Viburnum
Weigela

Santolina

Euonymus

Weigela

SPECIAL CUTTINGS

A few shrubs, such as clematis, sometimes root better if you use special techniques. These are some of the most useful methods.

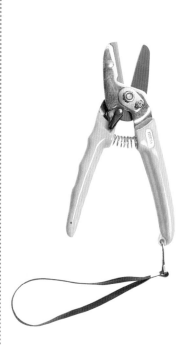

INTERNODAL CLEMATIS CUTTINGS

1 Take internodal cuttings to raise a lot of clematis rather than the smaller number achieved by layering. Remove a length of stem in the spring or early summer to cut into smaller sections.

2 Make each cutting by severing it from the stem *between* leaf joints (most cuttings are taken at a leaf joint or node). Leave about 2.5–5cm (1–2in) of stem below the leaves, with just a short stub of stem above the leaf joint.

3 Remove one of the two leaves, leaving a stump about 6mm (¼in) long. Leave the other leaf on as a convenient 'handle'.

4 Insert in the compost in the usual way. The cuttings will root more readily if you keep them in a propagator and maintain a humid atmosphere. Pot up the rooted plants individually and grow on for a season before planting out.

HEEL CUTTINGS

1 Some shrubs root better if the cutting is taken with a 'heel' of old wood – a slither of bark that remains when the cutting is pulled off. Evergreens such as rhododendrons and azaleas, and pieris, are among the shrubs that usually root more successfully if you take the cuttings with a heel. This method is also helpful for plants that have hollow stems, such as elders (*Sambucus*), and those with greenwood stems, such as brooms.

2 Remove the cutting by pulling downwards so that a piece of the main stem bark comes away with the cutting. The hormones that stimulate rooting are concentrated here.

3 A long 'tail' is not needed to root the cutting, so trim it off close to the base of the cutting, using a sharp knife. Insert the cutting in compost as usual.

4 Insert the trimmed cutting normally, in a cold frame, propagator or pot covered with a polythene bag. Use a rooting hormone on species that are slow to root.

RIGHT Juniperus cuttings usually root better if taken with a heel. Make them in early autumn.

ABOVE Cuttings are one of the ways that azaleas can be propagated, and some people like to take them with a heel.

LEFT Evergreen elaeagnus root readily from cuttings taken in late summer or early autumn. Leaving on a heel sometimes helps.

HARDWOOD CUTTINGS

Take hardwood cuttings in late autumn or when the shrubs are dormant. Most are easy to root and, because they are left in the ground rather than placed in pots, they need much less looking after than other types of cuttings.

TAKING HARDWOOD CUTTINGS

1 Choose shoots that grew during the summer but have now become firm and hard. Avoid very weak, thin shoots and those that are thick and old. Cut off the shoots with secateurs. They can be longer than the actual cuttings because you can take several from one shoot by dividing it into shorter lengths later.

2 Pull off any dying leaves that remain on the shoot, then cut it into sections about 15–23cm (6–9in) long.

3 So that you remember which end is the top, make a sloping cut just above the top bud, and a horizontal one at the appropriate distance underneath.

4 Choose a sheltered but not dry part of the garden to make a slit trench with a spade. Push the spade in vertically to the appropriate depth, then push it forwards to create an almost V-shaped trench.

5 To discourage water from standing around the base of the cuttings, which may cause rotting, sprinkle a thick layer of grit or coarse sand along the bottom of the trench before planting.

SINGLE STEM CUTTINGS

If you are taking cuttings of trees that you want to grow with a single stem, or fruit bushes with a single leg (stem), insert the cutting so the tip is just covered. This will discourage the growth of the lower buds on the stem.

6 For most shrubs, insert the cuttings so that only about 2.5–5cm (1–2in) shows above the ground. Insert vertically, about 10cm (4in) apart. Firm them in well.

Cornus alba and its varieties are grown mainly for their attractive coloured winter stems. They are very easy to propagate from hardwood cuttings.

ROOTING HORMONES

Rooting hormones – which can be powders or liquids – are most useful for plants that are difficult to root. They can be used on all stem cuttings, so you may prefer to use them routinely. However, they are not intended for use on leaf or root cuttings.

Most of the hormones will be taken up through the cut base of the cutting, not through the bark or stem, so you only need to dip the cut surface into the powder or liquid.

If using a powder, dip the tip of the cutting into water first, so the powder adheres to the cutting more readily.

Rooting hormones can be formulated with different chemicals and strengths to suit different types of cutting – such as hardwood or softwood – but most sold for amateurs are all-purpose.

Many contain a fungicide, which will reduce the risk of the cutting rotting before it has taken root.

Most rooting hormones used by amateurs come as powders.

Some hormones are dissolved in water or solvents, but those sold for amateurs are usually formulated as a gel.

PLANTS TO TRY

Most deciduous (leaf-shedding) shrubs can be propagated from hardwood cuttings. Popular ones that root easily from hardwood cuttings include:

Cotoneaster
Dogwood (*Cornus alba*)
Flowering currant (*Ribes sanguineum*)
Rose (below)
Winter-flowering viburnum

Trees can also be propagated from hardwood cuttings. Those that root readily include poplars (*Populus*) and willows (*Salix*).

LAYERING

Layering is an ideal way to propagate shrubs and some house plants if you need just a few extra plants. You will usually have a larger plant more quickly than you would from cuttings. Air layering is a good technique to use if you have a leggy plant that has become bare at the base. Simple layering is best for shrubs in the garden, but if you have a climber such as a clematis or honeysuckle you can use serpentine layering and root even more plants.

AFTERCARE

■ Water thoroughly and try to prevent the soil drying out before the plant has rooted.

■ Sever the stem from its parent in the autumn or spring (pull a little soil away with your hand to check whether the layer has rooted).

■ After severing it from its parent, pinch out the growing tip of the new plant to make it bushy.

■ Lift and replant if well-rooted; if not, leave for up to a year.

PLANTS TO TRY

Most shrubs and some trees can be layered if there are suitable low-growing shoots, but those that are often propagated this way include:

Corylus avellana 'Contorta' (contorted willow)
Hamamelis (witch hazel)
Magnolia x *soulangeana*
Magnolia stellata
Rhododendron (opposite)
Syringa vulgaris (lilac)
Viburnum

SIMPLE LAYERING

1 Choose a young, low-growing branch flexible enough to be bent down easily, and trim the leaves and sideshoots off the part of the stem that will be in contact with the ground. Leave on some leaves at the end of the stem.

2 Lower the stem to the ground and note the point about 23cm (9in) behind the tip where it comes into contact with the soil. Then use a spade to make a hole 10–15cm (4–6in) deep that slopes towards the parent plant but has a vertical end.

3 Hold the stem in contact with the soil using a peg of bent wire or a forked stick. If you do not have suitable wire, try cutting a length from an old wire coat-hanger. Make sure that the end of the stem lies vertically against the back of the hole.

4 Return the excavated soil to bury the stem, and firm it in well (use the heel of your shoe if necessary).

GARDENING BASICS

AIR LAYERING

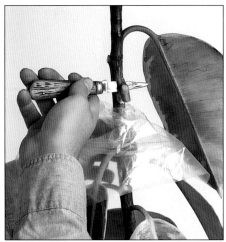

1 Trim off any leaves that are growing in the place where you want to make the layer. Make a polythene sleeve to go around the stem (you can use a polythene bag). Secure the bottom of the sleeve just below the layering point, which will be beneath an old leaf scar, using tape or a plastic-covered wire twist-tie.

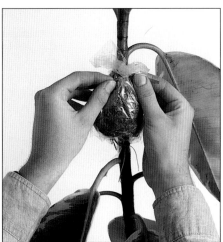

2 Holding the sleeve out of the way, use a sharp knife or blade to make a slanting upward cut about 2.5cm (1in) long. Be careful not to cut more than half-way through the stem, or the shoot may break off completely.

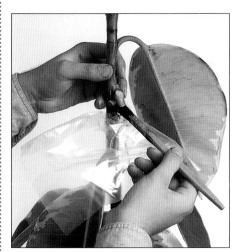

3 Brush a little hormone rooting powder or liquid into the cut, then pack with sphagnum moss to keep the wound open.

4 Pull the sleeve over the wounded area and pack it with plenty of moist sphagnum moss (try a florist if your garden centre does not have any). Secure at the top with more tape or another plastic-covered wire twist-tie.

AFTERCARE

■ Look after the parent plant normally and do not attempt to remove the layered section until you can see roots.

■ Once plenty of roots have formed, cut through the stem below the layered area. Loosen the ball of moss and tease out some of the roots when you pot it up.

PLANTS TO TRY

Air layering is most commonly used for indoor plants that have become bare at the base, but it can be used for garden trees and shrubs. Plants for which the technique is often used include:

Indoors
Ficus elastica (rubber plant)
Dracaena
Outdoors
Hamamelis (witch hazel)
Magnolia
Rhododendron (below)
Syringa (lilac)

SERPENTINE LAYERING

Strip the leaves from a healthy shoot at the points where the stem will be buried, leaving several intact so that the stem snakes in and out of the ground. At each joint, make a slanting cut about 2.5cm (1in) long and almost half-way through. Insert a small piece of matchstick in the cut to prevent it closing up again and pin down with a piece of bent wire. Cover with soil, and keep well watered.
Plants to try Serpentine layering is suitable only for climbers or trailers with long stems that can be pegged to the ground, such as:

Clematis (opposite)
Lonicera, climbing forms (honeysuckle)
Parthenocissus (Boston ivy, Virginia creeper)

Leaf Cuttings

Leaf cuttings can be fun to root, and are an ideal way to propagate house plants such as African violets (*Saintpaulia*) and Cape primroses (*Streptocarpus*).

Leaf Petiole Cuttings

1 Plants such as African violets (*Saintpaulia*) can be propagated from leaf cuttings taken with the stalk (petiole) attached. Select young but fully-grown healthy leaves and cut them off cleanly.

2 Trim the stalk about 3cm (1¼in) below the leaf blade and insert in a pot of cuttings compost, vermiculite or perlite, so the bottom of the leaf blade is just in contact with the compost.

3 Cover with a mini cloche made from the upper section of a plastic drinks bottle, or use an inflated polythene bag held in place with an elastic band. Label and keep in a warm light place, out of direct sunlight.

4 Keep the compost damp but not wet, and remove any condensation from the cover regularly. Pot up the plantlet that grows from the base as soon as it is growing vigorously.

Leaf Section Cuttings

1 The leaves of the Cape primrose (*Streptocarpus*), and some other plants, can be cut into sections. Use a sharp knife or razor-blade to slice the leaves into sections 5–8cm (2–3in) wide.

2 Push each cut section vertically into a tray of cuttings compost. Keep the side that was nearest the leaf stalk downwards, and bury about one-third of the cutting.

3 Keep the compost just moist and in a warm light place, out of direct sunlight. When small plantlets grow at the base, pot them up individually.

African violets are particularly easy to root from leaf cuttings (see leaf petiole cuttings).

LEAF BLADE CUTTINGS

1 Some plants, such as *Begonia rex*, will produce new plants from the leaf blade (lamina). Choose mature but healthy leaves, and retain part of the stem. With a sharp knife, cut straight across the main veins from the underside, making each cut about 12mm (½in) long.

2 Place the leaf on a tray of compost, pushing the stub of the stalk in to help hold the leaf in position. Use a piece of bent wire to hold the veins in contact with the compost.

3 Alternatively, hold the leaf down with small stones.

4 Label, then keep the tray in a warm, light place, but out of direct sunlight. Once small plants have developed, carefully separate them from the leaf and pot up individually.

DIVISION

Division is one of the quickest and easiest methods of propagation, and ideal if you require just a few extra plants. Many herbaceous plants benefit from division anyway once they have formed a congested clump of growth after some years.

DIVIDING HERBACEOUS PLANTS

1 Divide large clumps as the shoots emerge in spring. Use a fork to loosen and lift the clump.

2 Use two forks back to back to tear the clump into smaller and more manageable pieces.

3 If you want just a couple of large plants, replant without further division, but discard any dead parts in the centre of the clump. To make more plants, pull the pieces into smaller segments. Some are too tough to pull apart with your hands, in which case cut through them with a knife or chop into smaller pieces with a spade.

4 Replant the small pieces into prepared ground. Rake in a balanced garden fertilizer before planting.

DIVIDING FLAG IRISES

1 Divide rhizomatous flag irises that have become congested after flowering. Lift the clump with a fork and shake off as much soil as possible.

2 You should replant the current season's growth, so cut away and discard the old part of the rhizome.

3 Trim the leaves to about 5–8cm (2–3in) from the rhizome. This will reduce the amount of water lost from the plant while new roots are growing.

DIVIDING AQUATIC PLANTS

1 If a planting basket has been used, the roots may have grown through it. Cut the roots flush with the basket, using a sharp knife, so that you can remove the plant. Use a spade to chop the clump into smaller pieces.

2 The roots of some plants, such as aquatic rushes and irises, are very tough, and it may be necessary to cut through them with a sharp knife. Replant the pieces in fresh compost, placing a new liner in the basket if using the old one.

DIVIDING BEGONIA TUBERS

1 Start the tubers off in late winter or early spring in trays of compost in a light, warm place. When you can see the shoots beginning to grow, cut the tubers into several pieces, making sure that each one has a shoot or bud.

2 Dust the cut surfaces with a fungicide, then pot up individually in small pots.

DIVIDING DAHLIA TUBERS

If you require only two or three extra dahlia plants from your tuber, division is an alternative to cuttings. In late spring divide the tubers into two or three smaller clumps with a sharp knife. Always make sure that each piece has some shoots starting to grow, or buds. Ensure that there is a piece of old stem attached – isolated tubers will not grow. Alternatively, start the tubers off in boxes or trays. When the growth is a few centimetres high, cut through the tuber, making sure that each piece has a shoot. Dust cut surfaces with a fungicide then pot up until it is safe to plant outside.

4 Replant on a slight ridge of soil, spreading the roots either side. Cover the roots with soil, but leave the top of the rhizome exposed.

ROOT CUTTINGS

Root cuttings are usually taken in winter when there is not much outdoor propagation to be done. Several border plants and alpines root readily with this technique, which is an interesting propagation method to add to your repertoire.

TAKING ROOT CUTTINGS

1 Lift the parent plant with a fork to expose the roots, or scrape away enough soil to gain access to the roots without lifting the plant completely.

2 If the plant has thick, fleshy roots, cut some off with secateurs or a pruning knife, close to the main stem or root.

3 Cut each root into 5cm (2in) lengths. To enable you to remember which way up to plant the roots, cut them horizontally across the top, but make a sloping cut at the bottom end.

4 Insert the cuttings into pots of a gritty compost (such as a loam-based potting compost with extra grit added). The top of the cuttings should be flush with the top of the compost.

5 Sprinkle a thin layer of grit over the surface, and don't forget to insert a label, as nothing will be visible until the plants root a few months later. Keep in a cold frame or cool greenhouse.

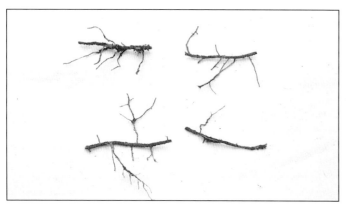

6 Some plants, such as perennial phlox, do not have thick, fleshy roots. In that case cut the finer roots into 5–8cm (2–3in) lengths, and do not worry about making horizontal or sioping cuts.

7 Lay the cuttings flat on the compost in a seed tray, then cover with compost.

PLANTS TO TRY

Root cuttings should always be taken when the plant is dormant – preferably in early winter.

Border perennials to try include acanthus, echinops, gaillardias, gypsophila, Oriental poppies (*Papaver orientale*), and border phlox.

Some alpines, such as the pasque flower (*Pulsatilla vulgaris*), can also be raised from root cuttings, as well as a few trees.

Romneya coulteri is an imposing shrub with flowers about 10cm (4in) across on a plant about 1.2–1.8m (4–6ft) tall. It can be propagated from 7.5cm (3in) root cuttings taken in mid winter.

PRUNING 1

Most shrubs require minimal pruning other than to remove dead or diseased shoots, but for some shrubs pruning will encourage better-flowering or more compact plants. The advice applies only to shrubs that have been established for at least a couple of years. Young plants may not require such severe pruning.

PRUNING FOR COLOURED STEMS

1 Dogwoods (*Cornus alba* and *Cornus stolonifera* varieties) and *Salix alba* 'Chermesina' (syn. 'Britzensis') should be pruned annually or every second year to encourage bright young stems like the ones shown here.

2 Prune in early spring, before the new leaves appear. Cut back each stem to an outward-facing bud about 5cm (2in) from the stump of hard wood.

3 The pruning will look severe when the shrub is cut back to a framework perhaps only 30cm (12in) high, but new shoots will soon appear.

PRUNING GREY-LEAVED SHRUBS

1 Small grey-leaved plants such as cotton lavender (*Santolina chamaecyparissus*) and the curry plant (*Helichrysum angustifolium*) need regular pruning to prevent them becoming straggly. Prune annually in the spring.

2 Cut back close to the base, to a point where new shoots can be seen. This may be as low as 10cm (4in) from the ground on plants pruned regularly, but to a taller framework of woody shoots on a neglected plant.

3 After pruning the plant will look like this, but new shoots will soon grow and by summer will make a compact, well-clothed shrub.

GARDENING BASICS

Pruning The Whitewash Bramble

1 A few shrubs, such as *Rubus cockburnianus*, the whitewash bramble, are grown for their decorative winter stems that arise directly from the ground like raspberry canes. Prune these annually in late winter or early spring.

2 Pruning is very simple. Just cut all the stems off close to the ground. If the plant is very prickly, like this whitewash bramble, wear gloves for protection.

3 The pruning looks drastic, but new shoots will soon grow, and these will be more attractive the following winter than if you had left the old canes on the plant.

Pruning Heathers

1 Prune heathers by clipping them with shears to remove the dead flowerheads. This will keep the plants compact as well as looking neater.

2 Trim the shoots back after flowering, close to the base of the current year's growth. Prune winter-flowering heathers in spring, and cut close to the base of the previous year's growth. Be careful not to cut into old, hardened wood.

Heathers become woody with age, with less compact growth and poor flowering. Keep their shape by clipping the dead heads off with shears after flowering.

PRUNING 2

Many shrubs, such as buddleias, need pruning every year. Others, such as brooms, will be better for a good prune. Slow-growing compact plants like cistus don't have to be pruned routinely at all, but it will stimulate the growth of more sideshoots and therefore more flowers the following year.

PRUNING DECIDUOUS SUCKERING SHRUBS

Deciduous suckering shrubs, such as *Kerria japonica* and *Leycesteria formosa*, will be a better shape and won't become too congested if you prune them every spring. Prune the flowered stems back to about half their original length, to a point where there is a strong sideshoot. Wait until flowering has finished if it's a spring-flowering shrub like kerria.

Remove about one-third of all the stems to within 5–8cm (2–3in) of the ground. Choose the oldest or weakest, or diseased or damaged shoots, to cut back hard.

PRUNING TO A FRAMEWORK

1 Plants that flowered the previous year, from mid summer onwards, *on shoots produced that year*, like this buddleia, need pruning every spring to keep them compact. All the growth on this plant was made after hard pruning the previous spring.

2 Cut back all the shoots each spring to within about two buds of the previous year's growth from the old stump. Long-handled pruners are best for this job.

3 This is what the plant will look like after pruning. It seems drastic, but the new shoots will grow rapidly and flower later in the year.

REDUCING NEW GROWTH BY HALF

1 Some shrubs, such as broom (Cytisus) and genista, still flower well if you don't prune them, but they become tall and straggly, with a bare base. You can tidy them up after flowering and prune to keep the plants compact at the same time. But you need to start when the plants are still young – you can't do much about a shrub that has already become bare and woody at the base.

2 Prune back all the new green shoots by about half the length of the light green growth. *Do not cut back into old, dark wood that has become hard.*

PRUNING SLOW-GROWING SUMMER-FLOWERING SHRUBS

1 Slow-growing and naturally compact summer-flowering shrubs, such as sun roses (cistus) and *Convolvulus cneorum*, that flower on sideshoots produced the previous year, grow well without pruning. But you can keep them shapely and stimulate more sideshoots and flowers by pruning as soon as flowering has finished.

2 Cut back the new growth – which is soft and pale – by about two-thirds. Always cut to just above a leaf joint or to a point where there is a young shoot.

PRUNING 3

Climbers sometimes need careful pruning to restrict their height and spread, and to keep them flowering well towards the base.

PRUNING A RAMBLER ROSE

1 In late summer, after flowering, cut out any very old, dead or diseased shoots right to the base, using long-handled pruners. Do not cut back the younger, healthy shoots.

2 Go along each of the remaining main shoots in turn and prune all the sideshoots from these to between two and four pairs of leaves from the main stem.

PRUNING A CLIMBING ROSE

1 In late summer or the autumn, cut out any dead, diseased or damaged shoots. If there are very old main stems, cut one or two of these back to the base of the plant.

2 On old climbers, cut one or two of the thick shoots back to about 30cm (12in) above the ground to encourage new shoots to grow from the base.

3 Work along each of the remaining main shoots in turn and reduce the length of all the sideshoots from each of them to about 15cm (6in).

PRUNING CLEMATIS

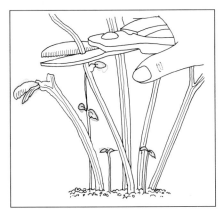

1 If your clematis flowers from mid or late summer, on growth produced in the current year, prune severely in late winter or early spring, before new growth commences. Prune all the stems back to a pair of leaf buds just above the previous year's growth – about 15–30cm (6–12in) above the ground.

2 This is what the plant will look like after pruning. Although the pruning seems severe, the new shoots produced will flower prolifically later in the year.

3 If your clematis flowers in early to mid summer on shoots that grow from the previous season's main stems, possibly with another flush of flowers in autumn, you must prune more selectively. Before new growth starts in early spring, cut back about a third of the stems to about 30cm (12in) above the ground, and also remove any dead or diseased shoots.

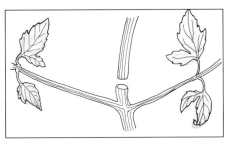

4 To restrict the size of the plant and encourage more flowering sideshoots, shorten the remaining long branches to a strong pair of buds.

5 If your clematis has relatively small flowers and blooms in spring or early summer, such as *C. montana*, prune only to restrict the size if it becomes too large. Immediately after flowering, thin or remove stems that are diseased, dead or causing overcrowding. Cut them right back to their point of origin.

RIGHT Most clematis that flower on old wood require minimal or moderate pruning, but those that flower on growth produced in the current year will become bare of flowers at the base unless pruned annually.

RUSTIC ARCHES AND PERGOLAS

An arch or pergola made from rustic timber is relatively simple to construct and is sure to look good with climbing plants. Leave the bark on or use peeled wood: it doesn't matter. If the bark is stripped there will be fewer hiding places for insects, however, and the wood is easier to work with.

Rustic poles can be used to make an attractive support for climbing and rambling roses, as well as arches and pergolas. The same basic joints are used.

A RUSTIC PERGOLA

1 A pergola must also be made to dimensions and designs that suit your garden, so plan it on paper first.

2 The easiest way to fix the horizontal poles to the uprights is to make a notch in the top of each upright that will take the horizontal snugly.

3 For a long pergola it will be necessary to join poles. Saw two opposing and matching notches as shown. Make sure that the joint occurs over an upright pole to support it. Like all the joints, fix firmly with rustproof nails.

4 Notch the cross-pieces by sawing a V-shape first, and adjusting it with a chisel if necessary. Nail into place with rustproof nails.

BELOW Clematis are often grown against a wall, but try growing them over an arch.

1 Sketch your design on paper before cutting any timber. A basic design is shown here, but modify it to suit the situation and height and width required.

Remember that you need to allow about 60cm (2ft) extra on the uprights to sink into the ground.

2 Assemble the pieces to your own design using a series of basic joints. This is a convenient and strong way to fix horizontals to uprights.

3 Where two pieces cross, mark the position and cut halving joints in each one. Use a saw and chisel to remove the section of timber.

4 You can use a wood glue for additional strength, but you will also need to hold each joint with a rustproof nail.

5 Bird's mouth joints are useful for connecting some of the pieces, especially horizontal or diagonal pieces to uprights. Mark the position carefully, then cut out a V-shape about 2.5cm (1in) deep. Saw the other piece to fit – some trial and error is inevitable. Drive a nail diagonally through the joint.

6 Assemble the sides on the ground first, then make the top separately. Insert the uprights in prepared holes and hold them in position temporarily with wooden struts. Drill and then screw the top into position. Nailing may not be stable enough for this position, and it may put strain on the structure before the uprights have properly settled in.

FENCES

Every garden has a boundary, and unless it's secure your garden is at risk. Walls and fences do more than just keep people and animals in or out of your garden, however, they can look attractive and can provide those vertical spaces so useful if you like climbing plants.

ERECTING A PANEL FENCE

1 Panel fences are easy to erect, and if you use post spikes you will save the effort of digging holes and setting the posts in concrete. Just buy a special tool to protect the top, then drive them in with a sledge-hammer.

2 It is essential that the spikes are driven in absolutely vertically, so keep checking with a spirit-level.

3 Once a post spike has been driven in, insert the post itself, and again check that it is vertical.

4 Lay the panel in position on the ground, to mark the point for the next post spike.

5 Drive the next spike in, and check that the post is vertical. Do not leave the post in position yet, otherwise you will find it difficult to insert the panel.

6 Panel brackets are the easiest way to fix the panels to the posts. Nail the brackets to the post already in position, and at the appropriate height on the next post to be erected.

7 Insert the panel, and while someone holds it in position erect the next post to hold it there. Then nail through the brackets into the panel to hold it firm.

8 Check both before and after nailing through the brackets that the panel is absolutely horizontal.

9 Finish off by nailing a post cap to the top of each post. This will prevent water soaking the top of the post and extend the life of the timber.

RIGHT Although panel fences are quick and easy to erect, there are plenty of other fence designs to try. Here, vertical boards have been nailed either side of the horizontal bars so that they overlap slightly.

WALLS

Tall boundary walls do not make a good DIY project unless you already have bricklaying experience. You will also have to consider strengthening piers for safety. A low garden wall like the one illustrated is suitable as an internal divider as well as a low boundary, and makes a simple bricklaying job with which to start.

MORTAR AND CONCRETE MIXES

For footings (wall foundations), and the foundation for a drive or pre-cast paving
1 part cement
2½ parts sharp sand*
3½ parts 2cm (¾in) aggregate*
*Instead of using separate aggregate and sand, you can use 5 parts of combined aggregate to every 1 part cement.

Bedding mortar (to bed and joint concrete or brick paving)
1 part cement
5 parts sharp sand

Masonry mortar (for brickwork)
1 part cement
3 parts soft sand

All parts are by volume and not weight. In hot climates, setting retardants may be necessary; in cold climates, a kind of antifreeze may have to be added. If in doubt, ask your builder's merchant for more specific advice.

1 Even a low wall requires a footing (foundation). Excavate a trench about 30cm (12in) deep and place 13cm (5in) of consolidated hardcore in the base. Drive in pegs as a guide for levelling the concrete. Check the level between the pegs at this stage.

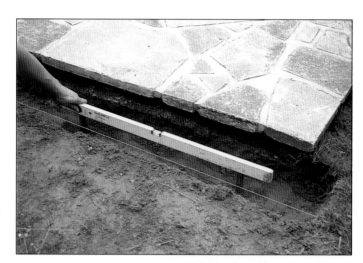

2 Pour in the concrete, and level it off with the pegs. Use a piece of wood to tamp the concrete level and to remove large pockets of air.

3 Leave the concrete to harden for a few days, then lay the first course of bricks. It is important to form a small pier at each end – and at intervals along the wall if it's a long one – as shown.

4 Continue to lay subsequent courses, first laying a ribbon of mortar on top of the previous row, and 'buttering' one end of each brick to be laid, as shown.

5 Use a spirit level frequently, and strike off any surplus mortar from the sides of the wall as you work.

6 Use the handle of the bricklaying trowel to firm and adjust the level of each brick as you lay it.

7 Finish off the wall with coping, and pier caps. This will make the wall look more attractive and also protect the brickwork from excessive moisture.

Bricks are a 'sympathetic' building material for paths and walls, and they can often help to integrate house and garden particularly effectively. A raised bed like this is a straightforward project to try, even if you have no previous bricklaying experience.

SURFACES AND PATHS 1

Along with the lawn, hard surfaces such as paving create the backbone of the garden. Plants add the shape and form, but paving has a profound effect on the visual impact of a garden, so it's important to take care to get it looking good.

LAYING PAVING SLABS

1 Whether it is a path or patio that you are laying, try to prepare a proper foundation. The depth of hardcore (rubble) needed will depend on the weight the paving has to support: about 5–10cm (2–4in) of hardcore is plenty for foot traffic, but if it has to take vehicles, increase it to about 15cm (6in). Remove the earth to an appropriate depth, allowing for the hardcore and the thickness of mortar and slab.

2 Compact the ground. You might be able to do this by treading it and banging it with a suitable improvised tamping tool, but a flat-plate vibrator like this is worth considering for a large area (you can hire one).

3 Add the hardcore, and check the approximate depth by using a straight-edge across the area and a steel rule.

4 Compact the hardcore by tamping it or hitting it with a club or sledge-hammer (this will also help to break large pieces).

5 Bed the slabs on five blobs of mortar – one just in from each corner and one in the centre. A mixture of 1 part cement to 5 parts sharp sand is suitable for most slab-laying jobs.

6 Place the slab in position, positioning it as accurately as possible, and lowering it down from one side.

7 Tap it into position with the handle of a hammer or mallet, using a spirit-level to make sure that the surface is even. If you are laying a large area of paving it will be necessary to lay it with a slight slope so that rainwater drains away freely.

8 Do not rely on using the spirit-level across just a pair of slabs. Angle it across other nearby slabs too, to ensure that it is level in all directions.

9 Some paving slabs are designed to fit with flush joints, but others are intended for mortared joints. Use home-made spacers to ensure a consistent gap for the mortar.

10 Fill the joints with a small pointing trowel. The effect usually looks crisper if the mortar is slightly recessed.

LAYING BRICK PAVING

1 The method shown here uses bricks bedded on mortar, but you can achieve a very similar effect (except for the mortar joints) by bedding clay pavers on sand. To lay bricks on mortar, prepare the base as described for paving slabs, but spread an even layer of mortar over the area being laid. If you lay the sides of a path first, it will be easier to check levels.

2 Lay several rows of bricks in your chosen pattern, pressing them gently into the bed of mortar. Then pass a piece of wood across the width of the path and tamp down with the handle of a hammer or mallet, to ensure that they are all level.

3 The easiest way to mortar the joints is to brush a dry mortar mix into the gaps between the bricks. Press down between the edges with a small piece of wood occasionally to make sure that there are no large air pockets.

4 Water gently from a watering-can fitted with a rose. Do not flood the area. Apply just enough water to clean the surface of the bricks and moisten between the joints. If necessary, clean any mortar stains off the surface of the bricks with a damp cloth before it dries.

RIGHT Bricks and plants look good together, as these petunias tumbling over the edge of a low brick edging testify.

SURFACES AND PATHS 2

Paths and other hard surface areas can be the dominant part of the garden design, so give as much thought to these as to the plantings that will eventually soften any of the hard outlines. Be prepared to mix materials, and to use different surfaces together: the stepping-stone path picture opposite makes an imposing focal point yet has the practical function of protecting the lawn too.

LAYING PAVERS

1 Clay pavers look like bricks but are thinner and are designed to fit together without mortar joints. Concrete pavers are designed in a similar way and are laid using the same technique.

After preparing a sub-base of about 5–10cm (2–4in) of compacted hardcore, mortar into position a firm edge to work from. You can buy special edging to match the pavers or use concrete edging like this. Check levels and adjust if necessary.

2 Lay a 5cm (2in) deep bed of sand. Make sure that the pavers will be level with the edging when laid on the sand. Adjust the depth of the sand layer if necessary. Use battens as a height gauge and to enable the sand to be levelled with a third piece of wood.

3 Lay the pavers in the required pattern, making sure that they butt up to each other and to the edging.

4 Use a flat-plate vibrator (which you can hire) to settle the pavers into the sand. If you can't obtain a flat-plate vibrator, tamp the pavers down with a club hammer used over a length of timber.

5 Brush more sand over the pavers, so that it fills the joints. Then vibrate or tamp again. It may be necessary to brush further sand over the paving, and vibrate again, to lock the pavers firmly into position.

LAYING STEPPINGSTONES

1 So that stepping-stones are comfortable to walk on, pace out the area to indicate where each one should be when you walk with a normal stride.

2 Lay the stones on the lawn, then stand back to make sure they look right visually. This is especially important if you want the stepping-stones to form a curved path.

3 Walk over the stones once more before you set them into the lawn, to make sure that the spacing feels right to walk on.

A stepping-stone path like this can take the eye across to another focal point or vista, as well as saving wear and tear on the lawn. In wet weather it will also protect your shoes.

4 Cut around the edge of each stone with a spade (or a half-moon edger if you have one), deep enough to be able to remove a slice of grass a little deeper than the stepping-stone.

5 Slice beneath the grass with a spade, then lift out the piece of turf. It does not matter if you dig a little too deeply as the layer of sand will even out irregularities.

6 Use a little sand to level the base and bring the stepping-stone to the right height. Make sure it is level and set just below the surrounding grass (if set too high it could damage the mower).

SURFACES AND PATHS 3

A large area of plain paving – whether bricks or slabs – can look boring. Think about creating a more interesting effect by mixing paving materials. And if you have a path to lay, a crazy-paving style might give your garden the kind of old-fashioned charm that it needs, especially if you choose natural stone or a sympathetic substitute.

LAYING CRAZY PAVING

1 Always lay the pieces dry first, concentrating on the large pieces and making sure those with reasonably straight edges go at the sides. You can fill in with smaller pieces once the key pieces have been arranged.

2 When the pieces have been arranged loosely, start to bed them on a mortar mix (1 part cement to 5 parts sharp sand is suitable). Use a spirit-level to keep the path as level as possible.

3 Use a piece of board across the width of the paving to help create a level finish. Tamp individual pieces of paving with the handle of a hammer or mallet if necessary.

4 Finish off by mortaring between the joints, using a small pointing trowel. You can add a cement dye if you wish to create a matching or contrasting colour for the joints.

MIXING MATERIALS

Do not be afraid to mix materials: railway sleepers and bricks or clay pavers look good together, gravel helps to soften the harsh effect of rectangular paving slabs, and rows of bricks can be used very effectively to break up a large expanse of concrete paving slabs.

RIGHT Combine pavers with a range of different pebbles to create an interesting surface.

INTRODUCING PEBBLES

1 Beach pebbles can be used to make a paved path more interesting, or as a device to absorb some of the gaps created when you have to lay a curved path with rectangular slabs. First create a bed of mortar, then lay the stones as closely together as you can.

2 Use a stout piece of wood, laid across the adjoining slabs, to ensure that the tops of the pebbles are flush with the paving (which will ensure they are reasonably comfortable to walk on). Tap the wood down with a hammer if necessary to bed them in evenly.

EDGINGS

A smart edge will put that finishing touch to a path, bed or border . . . and will prevent undue wear at the edge of a lawn.

1 Excavate a shallow trench deep enough to accommodate the edging. This comes in various sizes and designs – the design being laid in these pictures is known as a rope pattern.

2 It is essential that the edging can be laid flush with the path, so chisel off any mortar or rubble that protrudes beneath the path.

3 Gently tap each piece down with the handle of a hammer, using the eye initially to make sure they are level.

4 Back fill with soil, then compact it to ensure that each piece is stable. Add more soil and compact again until the edging is firm.

5 Use a long spirit level to ensure that the edging is straight. Small adjustments can be made by tapping with the handle of a hammer, but for large edgings you may have to add or remove soil.

FIXING A WOODEN EDGE

1 Unwind the roll, and if it is too long cut it to size. Use wire-cutters or strong pliers to snip through the strands of wire.

2 Decide on the height above the ground that you want the top, then excavate a trench of appropriate depth. This type of edging is useful if you want to create a low raised bed to fill with soil later.

3 If you need to join pieces, lay them in position then wire together. Make sure the edging is at the appropriate height, and reasonably level, then back fill with soil and compact it.

4 Lay a long piece of wood with a straight edge over the top of the edging, and use a club hammer on this to knock it firmly into place and ensure that the top is level.

LAYING A LAWN EDGING STRIP

1 Use a spade to form a slit trench along the edge of the lawn. Keep the back of the slit as vertical as possible.

2 Unroll the edging strip and cut it to the appropriate length. Lay it loosely in the trench to help judge this.

3 Back fill with soil, firming it without pressing so hard that you distort the shape of the edging.

4 Finish off by tapping it level with the handle of a hammer over a straight-edged piece of wood. Make sure that the edging does not stand above lawn level, otherwise the mower may be damaged.

A brick edging gives a smart finish to a path or lawn.

FLOWERS & FOLIAGE

No matter how well designed a garden is, with attractive features like patios, pergolas and ponds, it is the flowers and foliage that make a garden such a pleasant place to relax in, and why gardening is such an enjoyable hobby. In the following pages you will find plenty of advice on how to get the very best from your ornamental plants, as well as how to create features such as ponds, rock gardens and lawns.

OPPOSITE
Be flexible in the way you approach your planting. In this border there is a happy mixture of annuals and shrubby plants together with the herbaceous plants.

INTRODUCTION

Flowers and foliage are essential in any garden. They are the flesh that clothes the skeleton of the hard landscaping such as paving, paths and pergolas; they give the garden shape by softening harsh outlines, add colour and contrast, and provide a variety of textures.

The plants that you use, and the ways you combine or arrange them, are very much personal choices. Planting should express your own personality: the principles of garden design and planting 'rules' should only ever be treated as guidelines which you can then interpret in ways that suit you and the layout of your garden.

ABOVE Spring would not be spring without daffodils, but don't limit yourself to the yellow large trumpet varieties. There are many different kinds to try.

In the pages that follow there is plenty of practical help, whichever way you choose to plant your garden. If you are starting from scratch, however, make sure that you have the framework of the garden right first before you begin planting. It is much easier to undertake major construction or reconstruction work before the garden is planted. If you need a lot of plants, perhaps for ground-cover, or to fill a large border, it makes economic sense to propagate your own if possible.

After the 'hard' landscaping, make your lawns, or improve the existing grass. Lawns form the

ABOVE Use annuals such as cornflowers with traditional border plants to create an attractive 'cottage garden' atmosphere.

LEFT Tubs of colour help to bring life to an otherwise green area. The shrubby pink lavatera in the border is also a good choice, because it will flower for many months during the summer.

LEFT Few trees and shrubs have a long flowering season, so make the most of foliage effect. Here a purple variety of *Cotinus coggygria* contrasts with a golden form of *Sambucus racemosa*.

ABOVE Make use of hanging baskets to bring colour to a dull spot and to add a sense of height.

BELOW Antirrhinums and geraniums (pelargoniums) are two of the most traditional summer bedding plants.

largest percentage of the ground-cover of most gardens, so getting this area right will have an enormous impact on the overall impression of the garden.

When you plant beds and borders, balance your long-term aims with immediate impact. Plant herbaceous perennials and shrubs first, because they will take at least a year to start growing well, and fill in the gaps with plenty of bedding plants and bulbs for instant colour through most of the year.

And make sure you get the best from your greenhouse, which can become an interesting year-round hobby in itself and invaluable for starting off seedlings.

FLOWERS & FOLIAGE

95

IMPROVING A COLD OR WINDY GARDEN

If you have a very exposed, cold or windy garden, you are gardening with a handicap. By choosing suitable plants and using shelter belts and windbreaks, however, you can still enjoy the benefits of a beautiful garden.

PLANTING CONIFERS

Many conifers resent being planted with bare roots. It is better to buy small pot-grown plants. Buying small plants will keep the cost down and species that are suitable for hedging will soon grow tall.

PLANTING A SHELTER BELT

A living shelter belt filters the wind well and reduces its velocity so that plants within the garden can grow in a more protected environment.

ARTIFICIAL WINDBREAKS

Moulded plastic windbreak nets will give protection for five to ten years, or even longer. They are useful while hedges and living screens are becoming well established. Nail or staple the netting to stout posts, which should be about 1.8m (6ft) apart.

Plastic webbing should also last for five to ten years or more. It is a useful material for fruit and vegetable gardens where visual appearance is not so important. Stretch each strand tight, then staple it to the posts.

AVOIDING TURBULENCE

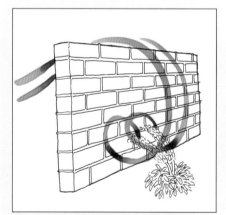

When wind hits a solid object, such as a wall or fence, it goes over or around it. Severe turbulence can be experienced a short distance from the leeward side, which can be damaging to the plants.

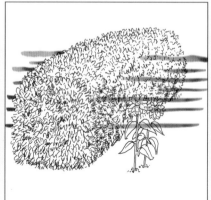

Hedges and screens of tall shrubs and trees are more efficient windbreaks, because they reduce the velocity of the wind while causing less turbulence than a solid windbreak.

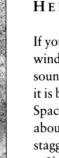

1 Prepare the ground thoroughly. This will be your only chance to improve the structure of the soil properly. Do this by forking in plenty of garden compost or well-rotted manure. Prepare a strip of soil at least 60cm (2ft) wide.

2 Break down any large clumps of earth before planting, and sprinkle on a balanced garden fertilizer (if planting in autumn or winter, use a controlled-release fertilizer, or a slow-acting one such as bonemeal).

SCREENS AND THICK HEDGES

If you need protection from the wind, or if you want additional soundproofing from traffic noise, it is best to plant a double hedge. Space the plants further apart, about 60–90cm (2–3ft), in two staggered rows.

If the site is very exposed, perhaps because you live on the coast or an exposed hillside, a shelter belt of trees will give more protection than a double hedge. Plant the trees about 1.2–1.8m (4–6ft) apart so that they will grow into each other.

3 Use a garden line to ensure that the row of trees will be straight, and insert markers at the correct spacing – usually 30–60cm (1–2ft) apart. If the area is very windy, stagger the planting of the trees, as shown.

4 Hedging and screening plants are often sold in bundles of bare-rooted plants, because this keeps the cost down when you need to buy a lot of them. Keep the roots moist and only separate them when you are about to plant.

AVOID FROST TRAPS

If your garden is on a slope, reduce the risk of creating frost traps by placing protective hedges at the highest level and leaving an opening at the lowest level so that cold air can continue to flow downhill.

5 Take them out of the bundle one at a time as you plant them. Dig a large hole for each one and spread out the roots.

6 Always firm the soil well to remove any large pockets of air and ensure that the roots are firmly anchored.

7 Rake the soil level, then water the plants thoroughly. Keep well watered for the first season.

PLANTING AND GROWING SHRUBS 1

Shrubs form a permanent framework for the garden and help to give it shape and form throughout the year. If a border of shrubs does not appeal, use them in mixed borders, or as specimen or focal point plants. Provided you get them off to a good start, most shrubs will give years of pleasure in return for the minimum of time and effort on your part.

BALLED PLANTS

1 A few plants, such as rhododendrons and lilacs, may be sold with their roots wrapped in hessian (burlap) or a plastic material. These are called 'balled' or 'root-balled' plants because they have been lifted from a field and their roots wrapped with a ball of soil. They are usually cheaper than container-grown plants of the same size.

2 Prepare the ground as you would for a container-grown plant, and check the depth of the planting hole as shown.

3 Once the plant is in the correct position and at the right depth, untie the wrapper and slide it out of the hole. Always remove the root wrapping, but try to disturb the ball of soil as little as possible.

4 Replace the soil, and firm it in well to eliminate large air pockets and to ensure that the shrub is stable.

5 Water thoroughly, then apply a mulch of chipped bark, garden compost or other organic material to conserve moisture and suppress weeds.

CONTAINER-GROWN SHRUBS

1 If planting a new border or group of shrubs, space them out on the ground while still in their pots. This will make it easy to adjust their positions.

2 Dig the ground, making sure it is free of weeds, and fork in plenty of well-rotted manure, garden compost, or proprietary planting mix.

3 Set the plant in the hole, still in its pot, to make sure the new soil level will match the old soil mark on the stem. Place a cane or piece of wood across the hole to check the level.

IMAGINATIVE PLANTING

Traditional shrub borders are often large, but you can plant a small border, and even a mini border, using dwarf shrubs. Choose a mixture of foliage and flowering shrubs, deciduous and evergreen, so the border has plenty of interest throughout the year.

In a small garden a mixed border can be very successful. Use the larger shrubs at the back and place herbaceous plants in front. Add some dwarf evergreen shrubs to provide winter interest.

Shrubs with a strong profile or bold shape, such as *Fatsia japonica*, yuccas, and phormiums, make good focal point plants. You can plant them in containers, as isolated specimens or groups planted in a lawn, or perhaps as a focal point at the end of a path. Use a bright flowering shrub as a

focal point to view across the garden against a background of less colourful shrubs.

Foliage lasts much longer than flowers, and in a dull corner or

shady border yellow leaves can be almost as bright as blooms. Group foliage shrubs together for an attractive picture through the summer.

PLANTING EVERGREENS

If planting an evergreen, shield it from cold, drying winds until it has rooted into the surrounding soil. Make a shelter out of a sheet of polythene or fine-mesh netting fixed to four canes.

SPACING SHRUBS

After five to ten years, most shrubs that you plant increase greatly in size, so initial spacing will be sparse or the shrubs will soon become overcrowded. Plant the main shrubs with final spacings in mind, then fill in with cheap, quick-growing shrubs.

4 If the roots are tightly wound around the sides of the pot, carefully tease out some of the roots to encourage them to grow out into the surrounding soil quickly.

5 Replace the soil around the root ball and firm it in well to make sure there are no large pockets of air that could cause the roots to dry out.

6 If the soil is impoverished, apply a balanced fertilizer around the plant without letting it touch the stem. Then water thoroughly and apply a thick mulch of garden compost, or a more decorative material such as chipped bark.

PLANTING AND GROWING SHRUBS 2

Established shrubs need little routine care, but weeding, feeding and mulching will keep them looking good. If you have planted a shrub in the wrong place, or if it has simply grown larger than you expected, it may be possible to move it to another part of the garden.

MOVING AN ESTABLISHED SHRUB

1 Quite large shrubs can be moved with care. Move deciduous shrubs when they are dormant. Evergreens are best moved in the autumn or spring. If the plant has spreading or prickly branches, tie them into an upright position to make the job easier.

2 Dig a trench all around the shrub, then use a fork gently to loosen the soil around the deeper roots.

3 If the shrub is large, it may be necessary to reduce the size of the ball of soil to be lifted. Use the fork to remove more soil, being careful to damage the roots as little as possible.

4 When the root ball looks as if it is a manageable size, use a spade to cut underneath it. Work around the plant evenly from all sides.

5 Make sure the new planting hole has already been dug and is large enough. Then roll up a piece of hessian (burlap) – tough plastic sheeting will do if you don't have any hessian – and position it against the root ball. Tilt the plant back and push the wrapping material underneath, rocking the root ball back over it. Unroll the hessian at the other side.

6 Tie the wrapper around the root ball, making sure it is secure. Unless the shrub is small, lifting it will be a job for at least one extra pair of hands. Get help before lifting if necessary.

7 Transport the shrub to its new home – on a trolley or barrow if necessary – and carefully lower it into the prepared hole. Make sure the shrub will be at its previously planted level, then carefully remove the wrapping material. After filling in the hole and firming the soil, water thoroughly. Continue watering in dry spells for at least several months.

WEEDING

1 If annual weeds have become a problem, and you want to avoid hand-weeding, some contact weedkillers can be applied provided you use a dribble bar to avoid spray drift and shield the stems and leaves of the plant with a piece of hardboard or something similar. Never use around newly-planted shrubs.

2 Some weedkillers can be used around established shrubs to prevent weed seedlings emerging. Use only around established shrubs, and in accordance with the manufacturer's instructions.

3 Hoeing and hand-weeding works well provided you do not let perennial weeds become established.

4 A mulch of garden compost or chipped bark will control weeds, provided perennials are eliminated first. Chipped bark can also be used to give a more attractive appearance to bare soil.

5 Established shrubs do not usually require annual feeding, but young ones will benefit from a general fertilizer applied in the spring. If an established shrub is performing poorly, try giving it a dose of fertilizer.

6 Some acid-loving shrubs, such as camellias and rhododendrons, do not do well on alkaline (chalky) soils. The leaves tend to turn yellow and the plants look sickly. Treating the plant with a chelated iron twice a year, will usually enable these shrubs to thrive.

PLANTING GROUND-COVER SHRUBS

1 Ground-cover shrubs, such as *Polygonum affine*, will suppress weeds after a few years, when they have grown larger and spread. In the meantime they will need help. Planting through proprietary garden matting is a simple and effective method. Eliminate weeds first, then tuck the edges of the matting into the ground to hold it in place. However, this technique is not suitable for plants that colonize by spreading shoots that send up new plants, because the matting has the same effect on them as on the weeds.

2 Using a sharp knife, cut through the sheet in the shape of a cross where you need to plant.

4 The matting will become hidden as the plants grow, but in the meantime you can improve the appearance by covering it with chipped bark or other decorative mulch.

3 Plant through the slit: this should be easily done with a trowel if you are using small plants.

Climbers need special care when planting as they often have to grow in poor soil that is usually dry because of the 'rain shadow' cast by the supporting wall, fence or tree. Take a little more trouble when planting climbers so that they get off to a good start. And provide a suitable support so that you can train them from the beginning.

AIM HIGH

Don't fix your trellis immediately above soil level. If you plant your climber away from the wall as advised, the shoots will need support only from about 30cm (12in) or even higher above soil level. It is better to fix your trellis with the base about 30–45cm (12in–1½ft) above the ground and benefit from the extra height that this gives you.

PLANTING A CLIMBER

1 Make sure that the support is in place first, then dig a hole large enough to take the root ball comfortably. The plant should be about 45cm (1½ft) away from the wall, where the soil is less dry. Fork over the base of the hole, and work in plenty of garden compost or well-rotted manure.

2 Position the plant so that it leans towards the wall at 45 degrees, and use a cane or stick to check that the root ball is level with the surrounding soil.

4 If the stems are secured to a cane or support in the pot, untie them and train the shoots to the wall support. Spread them out widely, taking them horizontally as well as vertically, so that the base of the plant will not be bare.

3 Tease out a few roots from the root ball, then return the soil. Firm in well to ensure that there are no large air pockets. Water thoroughly.

FIXING A BOUGHT TRELLIS

1 Expandable wooden trellises are suitable for lightweight plants such as large-flowered clematis, but are unlikely to be robust enough for a vigorous climber or wall shrub. Expand the trellis to the required size, then mark the fixing positions on the wall. Drill and plug the wall, allowing for the thickness of the spacers when calculating the drilling depth.

2 Use scraps of wood about 2.5cm (1in) thick, or proprietary spacers, to hold the trellis away from the wall, and fix with rustproof screws.

PLASTIC TRELLISES

Plastic-covered metal trellises suitable for clematis and other climbers that are not too vigorous usually come with the necessary spacers and fixing screws. If fixing to a brick wall, drill holes with a masonry drill and use a wall plug of the appropriate size.

PLANTING TIPS

■ To encourage your climber to grow away quickly, add as much garden compost or other humus-forming material as you can spare, before planting. It is especially important to add moisture-holding material to the soil when planting a climber, because the soil near a wall or fence is usually drier than in a more open position.

■ To conserve moisture, mulch the ground after planting and watering, using a thick layer of chipped bark or other mulching material. Make sure that the mulch is at least 5cm (2in) thick, but be careful not to bridge any damp-proof course.

PLANTING A TRAILER

1 Plants with a prostrate or low-growing habit, such as *Genista lydia, Cytisus* x *kewensis* and *Lithospermum diffusum* (syn. *Lithodora diffusa*), will tend to tumble over the edge of a raised bed more readily if you plant them at an angle. Set the root ball at an angle of about 45 degrees, growing towards the edge of the wall.

2 Trailers such as ground ivy and creeping Jenny (*Lysimachia nummularia*) will grow in all directions if not trained. Plant as close as possible to the edge of the bed, then direct as many shoots as possible so that they cascade down the front. Pinch out shoots that are growing inwards over the bed if these are likely to compete with other plants.

Even if your patio is wall-to-wall paved, there are ways to plant climbers to soften the brickwork, and you don't have to go to the expense of fixing a trellis. Use self-clinging climbers, or support with wires or special wall ties.

FIXING WITHOUT A SUPPORT

Lead-headed nails These are useful for securing small climbers such as rambler roses to a wall with old soft mortar. Drive them in with a hammer, then fold the soft flap over to hold the shoot.

Epoxy resin ties A modern equivalent of the lead-headed nail is the plastic tie that you 'glue' by mixing a special putty with a hardener and pressing to the wall. They are useful for climbing roses.

PLANTING IN PAVING

1 Lift one or two paving slabs next to the wall, using a cold chisel or bolster and club hammer to remove any mortar and break the slab to free it if necessary. Remove the sub-base of sand or concrete, again breaking it up with chisel and hammer.

2 When soil has been reached, tip on several bucketsful of garden compost or proprietary planting mix, and add a handful of slow-release or controlled-release fertilizer. Fork it all together, mixing thoroughly with the soil. A narrow border fork may be easier to use than a normal digging fork if the area is very small.

3 Plant the climber as described on the preceding spread. To make the planted area look more attractive on your patio, the soil can be covered with beach pebbles or fine gravel.

PLANTING A CLIMBER IN A CONTAINER

1 If you don't want to lift the paving, plant in a container. Wall shrubs and climbers will need a large container such as a half- or quarter-barrel, or a plastic shrub tub designed to fit against the wall.

2 Place a layer of rubble, gravel or broken clay pots in the base to ensure that water drains freely, then fill with a loam-based compost.

3 Plant firmly and water in thoroughly, then train to a support. Plant small-leaved ivies to cascade over the front of the container, or annual trailers like cascading geraniums (pelargoniums) for summer colour at the base.

SECURING CLIMBERS AND WALL SHRUBS

1 Very old walls that have not been repointed may have a soft lime-based mortar, in which case you can buy knock-in vine eyes (metal tags with a hole through which you can fix wire). It is likely that the mortar in your house will be too hard to allow this, so buy screw-type eyes and drill and plug the wall first. Stretch strong galvanized wire between the eyes. Space the horizontal wires about 30–45cm (1–1½ft) apart. This is adequate for wall shrubs such as pyracanthas and climbers like roses. For twiners like clematis fix vertical wires too so that the wires form a mesh.

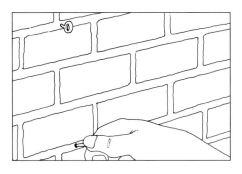

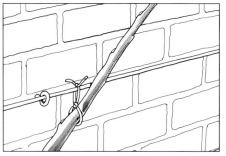

2 Tie the shoots loosely to the wires, allowing them space to expand. Use soft garden twine or proprietary plastic or wire garden ties.

RIGHT Honeysuckles such as *Lonicera periclymenum* are vigorous climbers, and will soon cover a wall or fence.

PLANTING TREES 1

Trees should always be planted with care. You have only one chance to get them off to a good start, so it pays to make sure you have chosen the right tree and a suitable position, then to plant and stake it carefully.

PLANTING A TREE IN A LAWN

1 Mark out the edge of the circular bed, using sand so that you can check the symmetry before removing the turf. Make the circle 90cm–1.2m (3–4ft) across. Push the spade in vertically around the edge first, then push the spade in at a shallow angle to lift the turf.

2 Remove about the top 30cm (12in) of soil, then fork over the rest thoroughly, working in plenty of garden compost or well-rotted manure.

3 Insert the stake before you plant, placing it on the side of the prevailing wind. Hammer it in, allowing sufficient space for the root ball.

4 If planting a container-grown tree, tease out some of the thick roots running around the inside of the pot before planting.

5 Place the roots in the soil, and place a cane across the hole to check that the soil mark on the tree's stem is level with the ground.

BARE-ROOTED TREES

Bare-rooted trees should be planted while they are dormant – between late autumn and early spring. Spread the roots out widely, making sure that the old soil mark on the stem is level with the surrounding soil.

6 Return the soil to the hole, and tread it firmly around the roots to eliminate air pockets. If the soil is very impoverished, rake in a slow-release fertilizer.

7 Water thoroughly, then apply a mulch at least 5cm (2in) thick to conserve moisture and keep down weeds. It will also make the bed look more attractive.

HOW TO APPLY A TREE TIE

1 Choose a proprietary tree tie of the type that has a buffer to separate the stake from the tree itself.

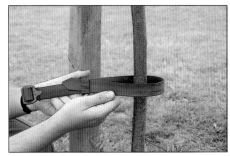

2 First loop the tie around the tree, then push the free end through the spacer. Make sure that there is enough free end to wrap around the stake.

3 Push the end through the buckle to secure the tie around the stake. Depending on the type of tie, there may be a loop through which you can tuck the loose end, but do not cut it off short, because the tie will have to be loosened every year as the tree grows and the trunk expands.

Secure the tie by nailing it in position. This will prevent it from slipping. Unless you have chosen a specimen that is unusually large for planting, most trees require staking only for three or four years.

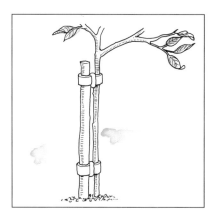

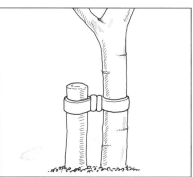

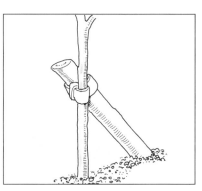

High stakes are best for trees that have long, thin stems while young, such as many crab apples and small standard trees. Make sure the stake is driven into the ground for at least 60cm (2ft); the top should finish just below the point where the branches start.

Low stakes are preferable for most trees as they allow the stem to flex more in the wind, which helps to strengthen it.

Angled stakes are useful if you have to add the stake after the tree has been planted – especially if a container-grown tree has been used. Drive the stake in at an angle to miss most of the root ball. Try to make sure the stake points into the prevailing wind.

Plant a tree in your lawn to suit the size of your garden. A small conifer is ideal where space is restricted.

FLOWERS & FOLIAGE

PLANTING TREES 2

Give your trees a good start in life: after planting make sure that they grow into an attractive and appropriate shape, reduce competition from weeds and protect them from animals.

WIND PROTECTION

Evergreen trees and shrubs will benefit from wind protection for the first autumn and winter. Fix windbreak netting or a plastic sheet around four canes or stakes, but leave the top open. Remove it in the spring.

FORMATIVE TRAINING

1 If you want a multi-stemmed tree or one with branches close to the ground, buy one with shoots along the length of the trunk. Prune out only those that are badly positioned, or crossing other shoots, and allow the others to grow. Shorten the remaining sideshoots to within 5–10cm (2–4in) of the trunk. Do this only once.

2 If you want a tree with a clear trunk, cut back all the new shoots above the branching head to about 10–15cm (4–6in) during the summer. When the plant is dormant, cut the shoots right back to the stem.

3 If you want a tree with a dominant central leading shoot, make sure that it has not developed two leaders – perhaps because the growing tip has been damaged. Prune one of them back to its point of origin, leaving the dominant or most upright leading shoot to continue upward growth.

4 Some trees – such as crab apples – are best with a rounded, branching head rather than a tall central dominant shoot. Remove the lower shoots to produce a clear stem, as described above. When the tree has reached about 60cm (2ft) taller than the required final height of the clear stem, remove the tip of the leading shoot.

CONSERVING MOISTURE AND CONTROLLING WEEDS

1 Trees will become established more quickly and grow faster if you ensure that they do not go short of water. Insert a pot close to the roots so that water penetrates to the roots quickly instead of running off the soil's surface.

2 An organic mulch, such as garden compost, pulverized bark or cocoa shells will conserve moisture, keep down weeds and can look more attractive than bare soil. Make sure that the ground is moist and weed-free before applying it. The layer needs to be at least 5cm (2in) thick to be effective.

3 Although less attractive visually, inorganic mulches, like this mulching sheet, are just as effective at keeping down weeds and conserving moisture. You can make the sheet look more attractive by covering it with a layer of gravel.

USING A TREE GUARD

1 If rabbits or other animals strip the bark of trees in your garden, protect new ones. Proprietary spiral tree guards are widely available and easy to use, but are suitable only for trees with a clear stem. Start at the bottom of the stem and just wind the guard around as you work upwards.

2 Use wire-netting to protect trees that are too small for a conventional guard, or that are bushy close to the base – such as most conifers. Insert four stout canes or stakes around the plant and secure small-mesh wire-netting to this. Interweave the cut ends to hold the netting together, and if necessary secure to the canes with pieces of galvanized wire.

GROWING BULBS 1

Use bulbs, corms and tubers imaginatively. Plant them as border fillers as well as in formal beds, grow them in grass where they can naturalize, and of course pot up some for the home. There are plenty of readily available bulbs to plant in the spring for summer flowering, so bulb planting is not just for the autumn.

PLANTING IN A BORDER

1 Excavate a hole large enough to take a group of bulbs and, if the soil is poor or impoverished, fork in garden compost or well-rotted manure.

2 Many bulbs suitable for a border, such as lilies and crown imperials (*Fritillaria imperialis*), need good drainage. Add a layer of grit or coarse sand and a sprinkling of bonemeal first.

3 Space out the bulbs, planting at a depth that will leave them covered with about twice their own depth of soil.

4 To deter slugs and encourage good drainage around the bulbs, sprinkle more grit or coarse sand around them before returning the soil.

5 If planting summer-flowering bulbs in spring, position with small canes so that you do not accidentally hoe or cultivate the area before the shoots come through.

LEFT Crocuses show the true versatility of bulbs. They can be used in pots and bowls indoors, in windowboxes and other containers, in beds and borders to bring pockets of colour when there is not much else out, and can even be naturalized in the lawn.

FLOWERS & FOLIAGE

PLANTING IN GRASS

1 Use a spade, or better still an edging iron (half-moon edger) as it makes a straighter line, to slice through the edge of the area to be planted.

2 Use a spade to slice beneath the grass, then fold back the turf for planting.

3 Fork over the compacted ground to loosen it. It's a good idea to add bonemeal or a slow-release fertilizer at the same time.

4 The bulbs, corms or tubers usually look best if they are scattered randomly and planted where they fall to give a natural effect. If the bulbs are small, just press them into the loosened surface.

5 Large bulbs will have to be planted with a trowel. Aim to cover the bulbs with twice their own depth of soil.

6 Fold the flaps back over the planted area, and firm them carefully. Try to ensure that the lawn remains level.

7 If the bulbs are large, you can make individual holes with a bulb planter instead of lifting the turf.

8 Most bulb planters are designed so that the core of soil is easily released.

9 Crumble some soil from the bottom of the core to cover the bulb, and discard any surplus. Then press the plug of grass back into the hole.

GROWING BULBS 2

For indoors in early spring, try growing hyacinths in a glass. But don't forget to look after your garden bulbs, then they will continue to flower for many years.

HYACINTHS IN GLASSES

1 ABOVE Buy good-sized bulbs, and choose prepared ones if you want them to flower early. Fill the glass with water so that the base of the bulb sits just above the water – it should not be in direct contact with it. Keep the glass in a cold, dark place (or a light place if you wrap the base of the glass in kitchen foil to keep out the light). Top up the water whenever necessary.

2 BELOW When the shoot is about 2.5–5cm (1–2in) high, and the bud is emerging and beginning to show colour, move the hyacinth into a light, warm place to flower.

PLANTING HYACINTHS IN A BOWL

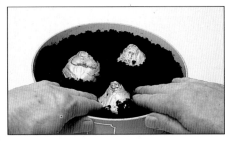

1 Partly fill the bowl with bulb fibre (you can use a potting compost if using a bowl or pot with drainage holes). Then place three or five bulbs in position so that the top third of the bulbs will be poking above the compost when the bowl is filled.

2 Water the compost or bulb fibre, then place the bulbs in a cool place outdoors while the roots form. Choose a shady spot, and cover the bowls with several inches of grit, sand or peat. If you slide the bowl into a polythene bag first, you won't have to clean off the covering material later.

3 Check the bulbs every couple of weeks, to make sure the compost has not dried out or become waterlogged, and to keep an eye on the emerging growth. When the shoots are about 2.5–5cm (1–2in) tall, bring them into a light but cool place indoors. Do not put them in a warm place until the buds have emerged from the leaves.

AFTER FLOWERING

1 Never try to force bulbs for a second year in succession. Plant them out in the garden, where they may bloom another year. Remove the old flowered stem first, knock the bulbs out of their bowl, and plant deep enough to cover them with soil – even though they may have been planted shallowly in bowls. Discard bulbs that have been forced in glasses or on pebbles; they are unlikely to do well after this treatment.

2 Resist the temptation to bend over or tie the leaves of bulbs in beds and borders. Try to let them die down naturally, and only pull or cut off the dead or dying foliage when it begins to wither. Otherwise you will reduce the chances of the bulbs flowering well the following year.

3 If you have daffodils or other bulbs naturalized in grass, do not cut the grass in that area for at least six weeks after flowering. If possible wait until the bulb leaves are beginning to turn yellow. Then cut them down with shears before mowing the area. In the meantime, be sure to dead-head them.

DIVIDING BULBS 'IN THE GREEN'

Some bulbs, such as snowdrops, may be sold or transplanted 'in the green' (with their leaves on), because the dried bulbs can be reluctant to grow. Lift an overcrowded clump with a fork and separate it. Replant the smaller bulbs where they are, and use the larger ones to replant elsewhere. Use a trowel or a widger to make the holes. Water in well.

DIVIDING OVER-CROWDED CLUMPS

1 If a large clump of established bulbs, such as daffodils, begins to flower poorly, overcrowding may be the cause. Lift, divide and replant. You can do this when the plants are dormant, but if you do it before the leaves die down completely it will be easier to see where the clumps are.

2 Separate the clump into smaller pieces, and replant some of the large, healthy bulbs in the same place. Either discard or give away the surplus bulbs if you have too many, or replant them elsewhere.

LIFTING AND STORING

1 Some bulbs, especially tulips which often succumb to pests and diseases if left in the ground, are best lifted and stored after flowering. Tender summer-flowering bulbs, corms and tubers, such as gladioli, need to be lifted for frost protection. Lift them carefully with a fork once the foliage begins to turn yellow. Remove the largest bulbs to dry and keep. Discard very small ones unless you want to keep them to grow on in a separate bed for a few years until they reach flowering size. Place the bulbs to be saved on a wire rack or sheet of newspaper in a dry place for a few days.

2 Shake the bulbs in a bag containing a fungicide. Then remove them, being careful not to inhale the chemical, and store in labelled paper bags in a cool dry place.

GROWING HERBACEOUS PLANTS 1

Traditional herbaceous borders are less popular in modern gardens than they used to be, but it is possible to use herbaceous plants in an original and imaginative way, even in a small garden.

1 Always prepare the ground by digging thoroughly, working in plenty of garden compost or rotted manure, and raking the ground level before planting. Space the plants out on the ground before planting. This makes it easier to adjust spacings if you decide they need planting further apart or nearer together. Try to visualize what the plants will look like when mature, and re-arrange them if necessary. Bear in mind that prostrate or ground-cover plants are best planted in bold groups, and other perennials will be better in groups of three or five of each plant if the border is large, rather than as individual plants dotted around when their effect may be lost.

PLANTING HERBACEOUS PLANTS

2 Make sure that all the plants have been watered about an hour before planting. Knock the plants out of their pots only when you are ready to plant.

3 Plant with a trowel (or a spade if the plant is large), and work methodically from the back or one end of the border.

4 Return the soil and firm it well around the roots, treading it with your heel to remove large air pockets if necessary.

5 Always water thoroughly unless the weather is wet.

6 If you buy root-wrapped plants (they might arrive like this from a nursery), keep them in a cool shady place, and keep moist until ready to plant.

7 Remove the wrapping at the last moment, and spread the roots widely in the planting hole. Water thoroughly, even if rain is forecast.

FLOWERS & FOLIAGE

ONE-SIDED HERBACEOUS BORDER

Traditional herbaceous borders are designed to be viewed from one side, with the tallest plants at the back and the dwarfest in front. This is still a good choice for a long, narrow garden where there is not enough space for an island bed. A width of about 1.2m (4ft) is adequate if you want easy access to attend to the plants. If possible, leave a narrow access path along the back.

HERBACEOUS PLANTS IN GRAVEL

You don't have to plant herbaceous border perennials in a traditional bed set in a lawn. If you have a gravel garden, try planting bold perennials like verbascum, acanthus, euphorbia or fennel.

GROUND-COVER

Many border perennials make excellent ground-cover plants, and once established will suppress weeds as well as look attractive.

Some, such as *Geranium endressii*, die down in winter but are very pretty for the summer. If you want evergreen ground-cover, try bergenias or epimediums.

ISLAND BEDS

Where space is available, island beds can be more interesting, with different facets of the bed being revealed as you walk round it. Place the tallest plants in the middle, with smaller ones radiating towards the edges.

PLANTING AN INVASIVE PLANT

Some grasses and certain other herbaceous plants, such as the decorative variegated pineapple mint, can be very invasive. Plant them in a large pot or a bucket to restrict their spread.

Make some *small* drainage holes in the base if none exists, then sink the container so that its rim is level with the surrounding soil.

Place potting compost or garden soil in the base of the container, so that the root ball will be at the required level. Firm the plant in well, adding more compost around the sides of the root ball. Finally, top up the compost to the rim so that the container is just hidden.

GROWING HERBACEOUS PLANTS 2

Most herbaceous perennials will grow for years without attention, but eventually they will need dividing and replanting. Some benefit from staking, especially in gardens that are exposed.

DIVIDING AND REPLANTING

1 Loosen the clump with a spade or fork and, if it's not too heavy, lift it on to the surface of the soil. Otherwise try to divide it into smaller pieces first.

DIVIDING FOR PROPAGATION

If you are dividing for propagation purposes, pull the pieces apart by hand into small sections, each with a shoot and root. Pot them up or grow them on in a spare piece of ground until large enough to plant in the border.

2 Divide plants with fibrous roots, such as Michaelmas daisies, or geraniums, as here, with two forks placed back to back. By alternately pressing the forks against each other and then in the opposite direction, you will soon pull the plant apart.

3 To keep the plant vigorous and flowering well, leave the pieces large. A large clump will easily divide into six good-sized pieces. Discard the centre of the old plant and replant only the vigorous pieces from around the edge.

4 Some plants, such as Oriental poppies (*Papaver orientale*) and verbascums, have thick, fleshy roots. If the clump is large, use a spade to chop it into smaller segments first, then divide the crowns carefully with a sharp knife. Replant groups of two or three pieces.

5 Small plants like polyanthus and pachysanora (shown here) can be lifted with a hand fork and pulled apart by hand, or separated with two hand forks.

STAKING PERENNIALS

1 Natural supports such as twiggy sticks are usually unobtrusive when the plants have grown through them. Insert the sticks while the plants are still just a few centimetres (inches) high, so the developing shoots grow through them. If the plant is a low-grower, bend over the tops of the sticks as shown.

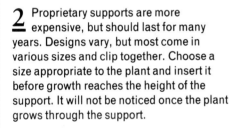

2 Proprietary supports are more expensive, but should last for many years. Designs vary, but most come in various sizes and clip together. Choose a size appropriate to the plant and insert it before growth reaches the height of the support. It will not be noticed once the plant grows through the support.

COMPACT FOLIAGE

Plants with compact foliage but tall flower spikes that are vulnerable to wind damage, such as delphiniums, can be staked with individual canes. Insert the cane and start tying the stem to it when the plant is about 20–25cm (8–10in) tall.

CUTTING BACK

1 Some plants, such as lupins and delphiniums, sometimes produce a second but smaller flush of flowers late in the season if you dead-head them immediately after flowering. Cut the flowered shoots off close to the base with shears or secateurs.

2 Even those plants that do not produce a second flush of flowers will look much tidier if you dead-head them. Some that flower early and have large, floppy leaves, such as Oriental poppies (*Papaver orientale*), will look better if you cut them back to the ground after flowering. New foliage will probably grow, but this will be more compact and won't overshadow neighbouring plants.

3 Cut back the dead flowered stems and dying leaves with shears at the end of the season. The border will look tidier as a result, and the rotting plant material is less likely to encourage overwintering pests and diseases.

KEEPING BORDERS BRIGHT

Shrub, herbaceous and mixed borders will all look better if you spend a few minutes each week smartening them up. Feeding and watering are often not essential, but the display will be more brilliant if you give the plants a boost.

FEEDING AND MULCHING

1 Feed your border plants annually if possible, and shrubs whenever they look as though they need a boost. Shrubs that are demanding feeders – such as roses – should also be fed annually. Follow the application rate recommended by the manufacturer, but sprinkle the fertilizer around the edge of the plants as shown – do not shower a powder or granular fertilizer over the leaves. Choose a balanced fertilizer and apply it in spring or early summer.

2 Hoe or rake the fertilizer into the top 2.5cm (1in) of soil. If you notice any on the leaves, knock it off.

3 If rain is not forecast and the soil is very dry, water the ground to help dissolve the fertilizer and make the nutrients available to the plants.

4 If some plants seem sickly and reluctant to grow, especially during the first few years after planting, try giving them a foliar feed. Wait until the sun has gone off the plant, then dilute a feed specially recommended for foliar feeding. Drench the foliage with a fine spray of the solution – what runs down won't be wasted, as the roots will also absorb it.

5 **LEFT** Mulching is not essential, but it will help to suppress weeds and conserve moisture, and it can look better than bare soil. A shrub border in particular will look better mulched. Apply a layer of an attractive organic material, such as this chipped bark, at least 5cm (2in) thick.

SPECIAL NEEDS

If you garden on a chalky soil, some plants will look yellow and need extra help. Lime-haters such as camellias and rhododendrons should be watered with a chelated iron (Sequestrene) at least once a year. Mix it with water, following the instructions, then apply it to the plant.

Herbaceous borders can begin to look untidy as the season progresses. Keep the plants watered and fed, and the ground weeded for a smart border like this.

WEEDING

1 Keep the hoe moving around the plants whenever you have the opportunity. Weeds compete with plants for light, water and nutrients, and of course they look unsightly. Hoe them off just beneath the surface on a dry day, and leave them to wilt and eventually die.

2 Deep-rooted perennial weeds that are already well established will probably regrow if you simply chop them off at soil level. Be prepared to dig down and remove the root completely.

DEAD-HEADING SHRUBS

Many herbaceous plants look better if dead-headed, but large-flowered shrubs such as rhododendrons and lilacs also benefit from dead-heading. With shrubs, be careful to remove only the dead flower in case you inadvertently remove the buds for the shoots that will carry next year's flowers.

END-OF-SEASON CLEAR-UP

1 Cut down the tops of herbaceous plants at the end of the season, unless they are of borderline hardiness, in which case they may benefit from the slight protection offered by the dead stems and leaves through the winter. Use a spring-tined lawn rake if possible, or an ordinary rake if not, to gather together all the cut stems, leaves and debris to put on the compost heap. If you leave them on the ground, slugs and other pests and diseases will make their homes among them.

2 Pick fallen leaves off low ground-cover and rock plants, otherwise they will block out the light and encourage diseases to flourish. You may be able to remove the leaves with a rake if you are careful, but if not remove them by hand.

PLANT SUPPORTS

Good supports will be almost unnoticed once the plants have grown, yet they can make all the difference to a whole range of plants . . . from floppy herbaceous perennials to climbers and vegetables such as tomatoes and runner beans.

1 The crossed canes method of support is useful for runner beans and sweet peas. Insert the canes in angled pairs, then slide a horizontal cane through the V formed at the top. Slide the cane down until all the angled pairs are secure, then tie to prevent sideways movement.

2 A wigwam of canes can be used for runner beans, sweet peas and plants like large-flowered clematis at the back of a border. Use three, four or five tall canes and push them into the ground at an angle so that they come together at the top. Tie them together firmly.

PLASTIC CANE GRIPS

Proprietary plastic grips can be used to hold the ridge of canes together. Designs vary slightly, but the one illustrated has two holes through which each pair of canes is inserted and the horizontal cane is then threaded through a special plastic loop. By pulling the loop through the grip, the canes are held firmly in place.

ABOVE Proprietary metal plant supports like these are useful for border plants with tall or fragile stems such as catananches. Position them early so that the plants can grow through.

3 Proprietary wigwam cane holders are quick and easy to use. Designs vary, but with this one you push the canes through the holes in the plastic ring. This holds them firmly and well spaced for an attractive wigwam.

SUPPORTING HERBACEOUS PLANTS

1 Twiggy sticks can be pressed into use as plant supports, but insert them early so that the plants can grow up through them. Push them in firmly to ensure that they are secure.

2 If the twiggy sticks are too long, especially if the plants are quite small and compact, bend over the tops so that they meet in the centre of the plant.

3 If you don't have a supply of suitable twiggy sticks, insert three or four canes around the clump, and loop garden twine or string around the plant.

4 A group of plants that tend to grow each with a single main stem that is fairly clear of leaves close to the ground, such as chrysanthemums, can be supported by a wide-mesh net stretched between four canes. Let the plants grow through the net, then raise it in stages as the season progresses. Alternatively, use a proprietary support, as shown.

5 Proprietary plastic-coated metal supports are more expensive to buy but will last for many years. These come in various sizes and can be linked together to suit the individual plant.

6 Sometimes it is only the tall flowering spikes of some border plants that require staking. Use single canes a little shorter than the length of the spike in full flower, and tie it to the cane as it grows. Alternatively, use a proprietary support.

CANE SUPPORTS FOR GROWING BAGS

Tomatoes and other tall plants grown in growing bags were difficult to support before the advent of proprietary cane supports. If the growing bag is placed on the patio or other hard surface, the shallow depth of compost in a growing bag is incapable of supporting the cane in an upright position. Designs for supports vary, but this one has three legs that are assembled using a base clip. When the support has been pushed through the growing bag from the bottom, a retaining ring is simply pushed over the top of the cane clamp. The cane can then be pushed into the clamp.

SUPPORT FOR WALL SHRUBS AND CLIMBERS

The best way to support a climber against a wall that needs a permanent support is to erect a trellis or fix support wires, but proprietary wall fixers are useful for perhaps a climbing rose if you do not want to knock nails in or screw into the wall. Designs may vary, but a popular make uses an epoxy bonder that you mix by working a tablet of adhesive between your fingers until it turns the right colour. This is then used to fix the plastic tie to the wall. After five minutes it will be dry enough to be able to tie the plant, but it is best to wait for about half a day if possible.

GETTING THROUGH WINTER

Many plants that would otherwise succumb to winter cold can be saved to grow another year if you protect them adequately. Frost-tender plants will succumb to the first frosts no matter where you live, but plants that will tolerate some frost may get through the winter unscathed in one area yet be killed in another. Take into account the type of winters you normally experience, and protect vulnerable plants if you are in doubt.

LIFTING DAHLIAS

1 Lift dahlia tubers once frost has blackened the foliage. Use a fork to avoid damaging the tubers.

2 Stand the tubers upside down in a dry, frost-free place. This will help moisture to drain from the hollow stems, and reduce the risk of rotting later.

3 Once the tubers are dry, pack them in boxes of peat, vermiculite, or some other insulating material, and keep in a frost-proof place for the winter. Remember to label the tubers individually if storing more than one variety.

PROTECTING VULNERABLE SHRUBS

1 Protect valuable shrubs of borderline hardiness with a winter wrap. Make a frame of battens or canes, and cover with bubble polythene or several layers of horticultural fleece to make a kind of tent.

2 Protect slightly tender wall shrubs with a shield of conifer branches pushed into the ground.

ALPINES

Alpines grow in areas where the winters are cold, but some of them are vulnerable to waterlogging in the winter – especially those with hairy or woolly leaves. You can protect vulnerable alpines with a sheet of glass held in a wire frame, or on bricks, above the plants.

STORING TENDER BULBS

1 Lift gladioli and other vulnerable corms and bulbs before there are penetrating frosts. Use a fork as this is less likely to damage them. Always dry off the corms and bulbs before labelling and storing. If you want to try using small cormlets or bulblets that have formed around the base, separate them to be stored separately. They will take at least two or three years to flower.

2 Dust the bulbs or tubers with a fungicide – or dip them into a fungicidal solution, then leave to dry again.

3 Pack in paper (not plastic) bags, or nets, and keep in a frost-free place. Don't forget to label them.

Summer Bedding

Whether you buy your summer bedding plants or raise them yourself, plant them with imagination as well as care. Do not plant them in the garden until any danger of frost is very unlikely, and always make sure they have been carefully hardened off. If you are in doubt about when to plant out, be guided by when your local parks department does its planting.

PLANTING IN DRIFTS

1 Plant in drifts for a bold effect, whether your garden is large or small. Bold splashes of colour often look better than lots of different plants mixed together. Mark out the basic pattern before you start planting.

2 Water the trays half an hour before planting, to ensure the compost is thoroughly moist.

3 Remove the plants carefully and space some of them out on the soil to make sure they will fit. Adjust the spacing slightly at this stage if necessary. Be guided by the seed packet or label that came with the plants – the amount of space depends on the type.

4 Dig a hole for each plant with a trowel, and plant it slightly deeper than it was in the seed tray. Pull some soil over the root ball so the seedling compost is covered – this reduces the risk of the compost drying out around the roots. Firm the soil well.

5 Water well, and continue to water regularly in dry weather until the plants look established.

TIPS FOR BRIGHT BEDDING SCHEMES

Dot plants, sometimes called spot plants, are used to give height and contrast to a bed of low-growing plants. These can be other flowering plants, like tall yellow African marigolds surrounded by red salvias, or silver-leaved foliage plants amid bright flowers. Standard fuchsias are sometimes used, but you can try any plant that is bold and contrasts well with the rest.

Carpet bedding (below) uses flowering and foliage plants to create geometric, abstract, or theme designs in a formal way. The plants are carefully positioned to make patterns. You can try this even in a small garden using dwarf bedding plants like fibrous-rooted begonias, lobelia, alyssum and French marigolds. Contrast with interesting foliage such as silver-leaved bedding pyrethrums.

Island beds look good planted with a formal design, with something high and bold in the centre.

Informal grouping (below) usually appeals to gardeners who dislike a formal approach to planting. Interplant one kind of plant with another, so that they grow into each other. Two, three and even four different kinds can look good together, more is likely to look confused.

Bedding plants don't have to be bold and brash, nor even used in traditional formal beds. Here they are in a predominantly white scheme in front of shrubs. The plants include white impatiens, silver-leaved bedding cinerarias, and pale-coloured pansies.

SPRING BEDDING

As soon as the summer bedding has finished, clear and replant the beds for a stunning spring display.

1 Lift the remains of the summer bedding plants, then fork over the ground. It is not normally necessary to add manure or fertilizer, but if the ground is poor apply a slow-acting fertilizer such as bonemeal.

2 Remove all the weeds and rake the ground level ready for planting. Rake in the fertilizer, if applied, at the same time.

3 ABOVE If you are using plants that you have raised yourself and have growing in a nursery bed, water them thoroughly about half an hour before lifting.

4 ABOVE RIGHT Lift the plants with as much soil as possible around the roots. If the soil is as damp as it should be, you should be able to press it into a ball to cling to the roots.

5 RIGHT Space the plants out to make sure that the spacing looks right before planting. Plant with a trowel, and firm the soil around the roots.

MIXED BEDDING SCHEMES

If planting more than one kind of bedding plant, such as forget-me-nots between wallflowers, allow plenty of space when you plant the first type. Then lay out the second choice before planting to make sure that the spacing is adequate.

Fully plant a small area at a time before continuing, otherwise it will be difficult to avoid treading on the young plants.

BULBS

Bulbs interplanted with spring bedding plants such as forget-me-nots or pansies look good and extend the period of interest.

Plant the bulbs between the young plants as you go along, to avoid having to step among them.

A LAWN FROM SEED

Sowing a lawn is cheaper than making one with turf, and it should soon become established if you sow at the right time – ideally, the spring or early autumn. If you sow during the summer, regular watering in dry weather is essential.

PREPARING THE GROUND

1 Level the ground by raking the soil to lines drawn 5cm (2in) down from the top of the levelling pegs. First make sure the pegs are level by placing a spirit level on a straight-edged piece of wood stretched between each of them.

2 Firm the soil by treading it evenly to remove any large air pockets. Shuffle your feet over the area, first one way, then the next.

3 Rake the soil to a fine, crumbly structure suitable for sowing seeds. Leave the ground for a couple of weeks to allow weed seedlings to germinate, then hoe them off or use a chemical weedkiller that leaves the ground safe for replanting within days. Rake once more to remove the dead weeds. The ground is then ready for sowing.

THE RIGHT TYPE OF SEED

Seed companies sell different mixtures to suit various tasks. Generally those containing ryegrass are hard-wearing, and those without ryegrass are for high-quality decorative lawns that will not take so much heavy wear. Modern varieties of ryegrass now produce lawns that look good as well as wear well.

These trial plots show how cultivation can be as important as the grasses used. The plots on the left are made from a good ryegrass mix, those on the right from a mixture without ryegrass. The top plots have been treated with a weedkiller, but the bottom ones have not.

1 Mark out the area into 1m (1yd) strips with pegs and string or garden twine. Divide each strip into 1m (1yd) sections as you work, using garden canes as guides. As you work along, lift the last cane to re-use for the next section.

2 Use a small container as a measure and mark inside the level of the appropriate amount of seed for 1 square metre (1 square yard). Apply it one square at a time, scattering half the seed over the area in one direction, then scattering the balance in the opposite direction.

3 If you have a large lawn to sow, it is worth buying or hiring a fertilizer and seed distributor. Check that it is delivering the correct amount by weighing what it drops on a sheet of polythene. Once it has been calibrated, simply push the distributor over the ground, making sure that adjoining rows touch.

4 When the seed has been sown, lightly rake it into the surface. If the weather is dry, use a lawn sprinkler to prevent the germinating seedlings from drying out.

Nothing sets off beds of flowers quite as well as a smart, well-groomed lawn.

A LAWN FROM TURF

Use turf instead of seed if you want 'instant' results that will give you a usable lawn within a couple of months. You can also lay turf at almost any time of the year provided you water in dry weather and avoid frozen ground. Spring and early autumn are good times. Prepare the ground in the same way as for sowing seed.

LAYING TURF

1 If possible, start by laying the first row against a straight edge, such as a path. Butt each piece of turf up close against the previous one.

2 Stagger subsequent rows like brickwork. Kneel on a plank to avoid indenting the grass already laid.

3 Roll the plank forward as you lay out subsequent rows.

4 Once the turf has been laid, tamp it down with the back of a rake, or roll the grass with a garden roller, to eliminate any air pockets.

5 Brush sieved sandy soil or a mixture of peat and sand into the joints, to help bind the turves together.

CREATING A CURVED EDGE

If you need to create a curved edge after laying, peg down a hosepipe or rope with lengths of bent wire. Then use this as a guide to trim against with the edging iron (half-moon edger). Use a sprinkler to keep the grass moist if the weather is dry. Be prepared to water regularly until the newly laid grass is well established.

6 Use an edging iron (half-moon edger) to trim the edges if necessary. Stand on a plank of wood to keep the edge straight.

MARKING OUT AN OVAL BED

1 A process of trial and error will be necessary to get the proportions right, but start by marking out a rectangle that will contain the oval bed, using pegs and string.

2 You can check that it is square by measuring across the diagonals, which should be the same length. Place pegs half-way along each of the four sides and stretch string between them, to form a cross.

ABOVE Make beds and borders look smart by ensuring a neat edge. Take special care when cutting out curved beds.

3 Cut a piece of string half the *length* of the oval (the distance from the top or bottom peg to where the other string crosses it). Use this to indicate where to insert another two pegs, as shown, using a side peg as a pivot.

4 Cut a piece of string twice the distance between one of these pegs and the top or bottom of the oval (whichever one is the furthest away). Make a loop from the string.

5 Drape the loop over the two inner pegs, then scribe a line on the grass while keeping the string taut. You will need to mark the line on the grass with sand so that you can see the outline of the oval. Cut out the outline with an edging iron (half-moon edger), then lift the turf inside with a spade.

ROUTINE LAWN CARE

Lawns usually take up the largest proportion of the garden, and they are often the dominant feature throughout the year. A neglected lawn can mar your garden, but one that is well cared for will set off all the other features.

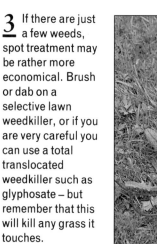

SPRING LAWN CARE

1 The easiest way to feed a lawn is to apply the fertilizer with a mechanical spreader as above. Alternatively, mark out the lawn with strings 1m (1yd) apart, and use canes to divide these into 1m (1yd) squares as you progress. Spread the fertilizer by hand at the appropriate rate.

2 If the lawn is full of weeds, apply a lawn weedkiller in mid or late spring. Use a watering can with a dribble bar, and mark off the lawn in strips the width of the bar. This will make it easier to apply the weedkiller evenly without missing some areas and double-dosing others.

3 If there are just a few weeds, spot treatment may be rather more economical. Brush or dab on a selective lawn weedkiller, or if you are very careful you can use a total translocated weedkiller such as glyphosate – but remember that this will kill any grass it touches.

4 Rake or brush off any debris and wormcasts. These will not directly harm the lawn but may provide a seed bed for weed seeds to grow in.

5 The lawn will look smarter if you trim the edges. Long-handled shears produce a very neat finish but are slow to use. If you have a large lawn, an electric lawn edge trimmer or a nylon-line trimmer with a swivel head will do the job more quickly.

6 If there are bare patches, reseed them before weed seedlings fill the space. Loosen the surface first, then sprinkle on some grass seed (you can buy small quantities of seed for reseeding small patches). Water well, and protect with a sheet of clear plastic until the seeds germinate.

FLOWERS & FOLIAGE

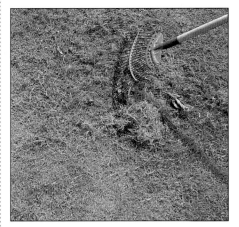

1 Rake the lawn with a lawn rake to remove the 'thatch' of dead grass and old clippings, together with any moss.

2 If you have a large lawn, a powered lawn rake will make the job much easier. This is quick, efficient, and will also gather up some of the autumn leaves at the same time. A powered slitter, like the one above, is useful for aerating a large lawn.

3 After raking, aerate the lawn. A special aerator that removes cores of soil is ideal, but for a small lawn you can manage with a fork. Push the prongs about 15cm (6in) deep into the ground, in rows about 8–15cm (3–6in) apart.

4 If your soil is heavy clay, brush sand into the holes created. If your soil is sandy, brush in peat instead.

5 If the lawn looks in poor condition, apply an autumn lawn fertilizer. Use one specially formulated for autumn use, and not a spring or summer feed, which will be too high in nitrogen (and encourage fresh young growth which will be killed by the frost).

6 If moss is a problem, use a moss killer recommended for autumn use. Lawn sand, sometimes used to kill moss, contains a nitrogenous fertilizer and is unsuitable at this time of year.

7 Improve the appearance of the lawn by straightening any uneven edges. Use an edging iron (half-moon edger) against a straight length of timber. Do not do this unneccessarily, because each time you do it you will reduce the size of the lawn slightly.

FLOWERS & FOLIAGE

DEALING WITH LAWN PROBLEMS

Humps and hollows that make mowing difficult, and broken edges that make the lawn look unsightly, can all be put right with repairs that leave it looking as good as new.

REDUCING WEAR

Protect an area that receives a lot of concentrated wear, perhaps beneath a child's swing, by pegging down a piece of thick large-mesh plastic or plastic-covered netting. The grass will grow through it but the netting will help reduce the wear on the actual surface.

BUMPS AND HOLLOWS

1 Use an edging iron (half-moon edger) – or a spade if you don't have one – to cut a cross through the middle of the affected area. Extend the cuts to the level area beyond the bump or hollow.

2 Use a spade to slice through the soil beneath the grass, so that you can lift it up to roll it back.

3 Roll back the four cut pieces to expose the soil beneath.

4 Remove soil if you are treating a bump, or top up with fine soil if you are levelling a hollow.

5 Level the soil as accurately as possible, then roll back the turf. If the level does not seem correct, lift the affected part and adjust accordingly at this stage.

6 Firm the grass with the back of a spade, or tread it in by distributing your weight over a plank. Then trickle and brush fine soil into the joints where the grass has been replaced. Finally, water well if the weather is dry.

FLOWERS & FOLIAGE

134

REPAIRING A BROKEN EDGE

1 Use an edging iron (half-moon edger) or a spade to cut a rectangle around the affected area.

2 Push a spade under the rectangle of grass, starting from the edge and keeping the slice of grass as even as possible. Try not to make it thick at one end and thin at the other.

3 Reverse the turf, so that the broken edge is on the inside, then fill the hole with sifted soil, and firm it down well.

4 Sow grass seed in the patched area, matching the type of grass if possible.

5 Brush sifted soil into the joints to help the grass knit together quickly.

6 After watering, cover the reseeded patch with a sheet of clear plastic until the seed has germinated.

ROCK GARDENS 1

Provided you can find a sunny site, even a small rock garden will enable you to grow a large collection of plants in a small space. With an island bed you can even make a rock garden in your lawn, or build one in a suitable corner of the garden.

MAKING A ROCK GARDEN

1 Choose a sunny site for your rock garden – sloping ground is an advantage but you can construct it on flat ground by building up a mound. Fork over the ground and carefully remove all weeds, paying special attention to perennials.

2 Unless the drainage is already very good, lay a 15cm (6in) layer of hardcore such as broken bricks as a foundation. For a raised mound like this, just tip garden soil or rubble over the area to a depth of about 15–30cm (6–12in).

3 Cover the low mound of garden soil or rubble with inverted turves, to provide a base for the special soil mix.

4 Although you can use ordinary garden soil, your alpine plants will prefer a mixture of equal parts soil, coarse grit and peat (or peat substitute). This will suit the majority of plants.

5 Mix the three ingredients thoroughly, turning them until they have been blended together.

6 Mark out the area you want the final rock garden to occupy with string or cord, and heap the soil mixture to the height of the second layer of rocks.

7 Remove the string or cord marking the shape, then start laying the rocks by placing a row of them all round at ground level. Add more soil around the sides and back of the rocks to ensure that they are perfectly stable.

8 Add the second layer of rocks, being careful to keep the strata (grain of the rock) running in the same direction. This will make them look more like natural rock outcrops. Use a crowbar or pole to lever heavy rocks into position.

FLOWERS & FOLIAGE

9 Try not to move heavy rocks without aid. Use rollers and levers to move and manipulate them.

10 As each layer is built up, add more of the soil mixture. This will consolidate the rocks already laid, and increase the height for the next row.

11 Make sure that the sides slope and build up towards a reasonably flat summit. Save a suitably large and nicely shaped piece of rock to lay on the top.

12 Finish off with a layer of coarse sand or – better still – horticultural grit.

13 The rock garden will look much better if it is situated in a corner like this one, with a backdrop of plants such as dwarf conifers.

ROCK GARDENS 2: PLANTING AND CARE

A rock garden can soon look neglected unless you plant appropriately and avoid over-rampant plants. Trim back plants whenever necessary, and make sure that weeds are kept under control.

PLANTING A ROCK GARDEN

1 Space out the plants in their pots before you start to plant. This will enable you to visualize what they will look like, and at this stage it is easy to move them around if the positioning does not seem right.

2 Water the plants and let them drain before planting. Knock each plant out of its pot by inverting it while holding your hand over the root ball. If necessary, tap the edge of the pot on a rock to loosen it.

3 Excavate a hole a little larger than the root ball. A trowel with a narrow blade is particularly useful for planting in the small crevices of a rock garden.

4 Trickle some gritty soil around the roots, making sure that the crown of the plant is not buried too deeply.

5 After firming, trickle more coarse grit around the plant, taking great care to keep it off the leaves.

6 Firm and level the grit to create a pleasing finish.

FLOWERS & FOLIAGE

138

KEEPING THE PLANTS LOOKING GOOD

1 Always remove weeds while they are still small, otherwise they will smother the smaller alpines. Hand-weeding is usually effective if done while the weeds are still small.

2 **RIGHT** If pervasive perennial weeds have grown beneath the rocks, it may be difficult to eradicate them by hand-weeding. Try painting on a translocated weedkiller such as glyphosate, which should kill the roots as well as the leaves. Be very careful not to let this weedkiller touch the plants you want to keep. You can also buy a selective weedkiller to kill difficult-to-eradicate grasses in the rock garden. This should be safe to use among most rock plants, but follow the manufacturer's instructions carefully.

3 If slugs and snails are a problem, sprinkle a few slug pellets around susceptible plants. Dressing the soil with coarse grit or stone chippings will help to deter these pests.

STONE CHIPPING DRESSINGS

A dressing of stone chippings on a rock garden will eventually need renewing or topping up. Some stones get washed away and the soil beneath gradually works its way through. If necessary, top up the coarse grit, gravel or stone chippings, using the same kind as before. Make sure that you place some beneath the collar of each plant, so that the leaves and stems are kept off wet soil.

CUTTING BACK

Go over shrubby plants in the spring and cut out any dead shoots killed during the winter. Many alpines, but particularly the vigorous ones such as aubrieta and rock roses (helianthemums), will remain more compact and vigorous if you cut off the dead flowering shoots with shears.

Planting In Walls And Paving Crevices

Make the most of all available planting spaces by packing a dry wall with interesting alpines and planting between the paving too.

PLANTING IN PAVING

1 Chisel out a few planting crevices if your crazy-paving path is mortared. Chisel out to a depth of at least 5cm (2in).

2 If you have a path with suitable ready-made crevices, clear out the old dirt and soil. Fill with a loam-based compost leaving space to plant.

3 Use small plants – seedlings or recently rooted cuttings – and tease away most of the compost to make insertion easier.

4 Trickle more loam-based compost around the roots after planting.

5 Firm gently with your fingers to remove pockets of air.

6 Water carefully. A fine mist from a compression sprayer is less likely to wash away the compost than a watering can. Water regularly, but avoid a forceful jet of water until the plants are well established.

7 Try sowing seeds of suitable alpines, such as dwarf campanulas, directly into the crevices. Clear out the crevice and fill with a loam-based seed compost, then sprinkle on a few seeds. Cover with a little compost, then water with a fine mist.

FLOWERS & FOLIAGE

140

Planting A Dry Stone Wall

1 Plant small seedlings or cuttings in the crevices. Even small spaces can be planted this way.

2 Press moist compost into the crevice to cover the roots. If the crevice is deep, use a tool such as a small dibber, pencil or garden knife to press the compost in to avoid air pockets. For shallow crevices you can use your fingers.

3 If the compost tends to fall out, try wedging a few small stones into the crevice to help hold it in.

4 Keep the plants and compost moist until established by spraying with a fine mist from a compression sprayer. Once established the plants will not require regular watering.

5 Try sowing a few alpines directly into the wall. Mix the seed with some compost in your hand.

6 Moisten the seed/compost mixture and press it into suitable crevices. This is most likely to be successful if you choose robust alpines such as aubrieta and *Alyssum saxatile*.

Many choice alpines can be grown in crevices in the side of a dry stone wall, but even if the wall is mortared you can create a similar effect by planting vigorous trailers and tumblers like aubrieta in the top so that they can spill over the edge.

A Garden For Wildlife

If you enjoy wildlife, modify your garden to encourage birds, butterflies and other creatures that will add to the beauty and interest of flowers. And instead of regarding all wild flowers as weeds, look on them as food sources for wildlife . . . many of them are as pretty as cultivated plants.

SOWING AND PLANTING WILD FLOWERS

1 The easiest way to produce a wild flower meadow, or an area of natural grasses and flowers in a smaller garden, is to sow a special mixture on prepared ground. Wild flower specialists provide mixtures that will grow well together, and starting from scratch means that the wild flowers find it easier to become established.

2 Specialist nurseries sell wild flower plants, sometimes as collections for a particular purpose. Buy these if you want to save time and trouble.

LONG GRASS AND WILD FLOWERS

Leave part of your lawn unmown and unweeded. On a large lawn this will add areas of 'texture', and will look acceptable on a small lawn if you leave it long around a tree or in one corner. You can cut pathways through it with a mower. Cut with hand shears in the autumn anyway, once the flowers have finished blooming.

3 Plant the seedlings as soon as possible after unpacking or lifting, in a position appropriate to the plant.

NURSERY-BED WILD FLOWERS

If you want to grow wild flowers in an established lawn, or plant them in wild areas of the garden, sow the seeds like cultivated plants and grow the seedlings in a nursery bed until large enough to plant. Lift them in spring or autumn.

You can buy wild flower seed mixtures that are every bit as bright and colourful as many highly bred plants . . . and you'll attract plenty of wildlife too.

MAKING A MINI-POND

▌ If you don't have a proper pond, make a mini-pool to encourage a whole range of pondlife. Birds too will visit.

You can make one out of a half-barrel . . . or even a plastic shrub tub without drainage holes. You can leave the pond above the ground, or sink it into the soil – which will make it easier for wildlife visitors to gain access.

Make sure that the container is level if plunging into the ground, and leave the top just above soil level to reduce the risk of surrounding soil falling in. If it has dried out and is no longer watertight, line the barrel with a pond liner, or fill any leaking cracks with an aquarium sealing mastic.

▌ You can even make a mini-pool for birds and animals to drink from with an old dustbin lid. Sink it flush with the ground, and mask the edge with stones or plants. Keep it topped up with water throughout the summer.

WINDOWBOXES

Make a really bold box with a single-colour or single-subject planting, or make it subdued and tasteful with foliage predominating, or if you prefer choose a traditional mixed planting of summer bedding. But don't leave your windowboxes empty at the end of the autumn – this is the time to plant them up with plenty of spring bulbs.

PLANTING A SUMMER WINDOWBOX

1 Place a layer of broken clay pots or pieces of broken expanded polystyrene over the drainage holes. If you don't have either of these, use coarsely chipped bark (sold for mulching).

2 Partly fill the box with a good compost. Unless weight is a problem, a loam-based compost is easier to manage as it is less prone to drying out and starvation. You can also add some water-absorbing crystals (*see* Planting a Hanging Basket) if you tend to neglect watering.

3 Buy pot-grown plants if possible. They cost more, but you do not need many for a windowbox and they make better plants more quickly. Space the plants while still in their pots to see how they will look. Adjust the spacing if necessary. If using foliage plants such as grey-leaved cinerarias to add contrast, use several, spaced along the box – one plant in the middle often looks like a mistake.

4 Make sure the plants have been watered first, then knock them out of their pots and plant. Finally, trickle compost between them to fill any gaps. Firm gently. Water thoroughly after planting, then place the windowbox in position.

PLANTING A SPRING WINDOWBOX

1 Bulbs require less feeding than summer plants while they are in the box. You can re-use some of the old compost from the summer, mixing it with some fresh compost to make up the volume. But remove the contents of the box completely and wash out the box with a garden disinfectant first.

2 Place pieces of broken clay pots, broken expanded polystyrene or coarsely chipped bark over the holes to allow for drainage.

3 Add just enough compost to cover the bottom couple of centimetres (inches).

4 Place larger bulbs, such as daffodils, at this deeper level.

5 Add more compost so that the larger bulbs are almost covered. Then plant smaller bulbs such as scillas, *Anemone blanda* or crocuses between them. Cover with more compost.

6 If you want to add a few pansies or forget-me-nots to make the box look less bare during the winter, plant these before finally topping up with compost. Don't worry about spacings if you are growing them with tall bulbs – the bulbs will just grow through them.

HANGING BASKETS

While you are planting out your windowboxes, be sure to plant a few hanging baskets too – they're challenging but make a real welcome by the front door.

PLANTING A HANGING BASKET

1 Line the basket with damp sphagnum moss, up to the level of where the first row of plants will be placed. If you find moss difficult to obtain, use a proprietary basket liner (*see* Basket Liners).

2 Although they are no substitute for regular watering, you can add water-absorbing crystals to the compost to act as a buffer if you forget to water as often as you should.

3 Add compost to the level of the moss, then insert young seedlings through the edge of the mesh. Try to keep as much compost as possible around the roots. If possible, thread the stem through from the inside, leaving the root ball undamaged.

4 Add more moss and compost – planting another layer if the basket is large – then fill to just below the rim. Put a bold plant in the centre if growing a mixed basket.

5 Fill in around the central plant. Water thoroughly. *Do not hang up immediately*. Keep the basket in a sheltered place, for a week or two until the plants are established.

PLANTING A HALF-BASKET

1 Line with moss and plant the sides as described for a normal basket. You may find it helpful to prop the basket on small pots while planting.

2 Plant the top last, then hang the basket on a wall – in a sheltered spot outside if you don't have a conservatory or porch. When it has been established for a week or two, move it to its final position – provided there is no risk of frost if you have chosen tender bedding plants.

BASKET LINERS

Moss makes an attractive liner, but many proprietary liners are available. Most of these look unattractive initially, but once the plants bush out you should hardly notice them. Choose one that makes side planting possible unless you want to plant only in the top.

Once the plants are fully established, take the basket to display outside. Baskets are usually suspended by chains hung on a bracket which can be securely mounted to a fence post.

TUBS AND TROUGHS

Tubs and troughs will add colour to dull parts of the patio, and they can be used to soften the effect of a flight of wide steps or to bring life to a balcony. Try planting a permanent container with a selection of year-round interest plants such as alpines.

PLANTING A TUB OR URN

1 Place pieces of broken clay pot, or coarsely chipped bark, on the base of the container. This will prevent the soil washing away through the drainage holes.

2 If weight is a problem, such as on a balcony, use a peat-based compost, otherwise use a loam-based compost. Partly fill the container, but do not top it up.

3 Whether using perennials or summer bedding plants, place a tall or bold plant in the centre, as the focal point.

4 Plant some trailers around the edge to take the eye downwards, unless the container is so decorative that you do not want to detract from its design. Small-leaved ivies are a good choice for a perennial planting, but if planting summer bedding you could use a flowering trailer.

5 Top up your container with compost after planting, and water thoroughly. A dressing of cocoa shells or chipped bark will improve the appearance until the plants bush out and cover the compost.

MOVING TUBS

Reconstituted stone and concrete tubs and urns are very heavy. Always get help to move them, and if necessary use a barrow or piece of wood on wheels to take some of the weight.

RIGHT A decorative tub can enhance the display of flowers. Don't spoil the effect with too many long trailers. This one is planted with pelargoniums (geraniums), a fuchsia, and *Helichrysum petiolatum*.

PLANTING AN ALPINE TROUGH

1 Choose pot-grown plants and, if possible, an attractive trough. Place a layer of broken clay pots or chipped bark in the bottom and top up with some gritty loam-based compost. Space the plants out to see how they look before planting.

2 Knock the plants out of the pots. If you buy alpines in large pots, it may be necessary to remove some of the compost from the bottom of each root ball. Make sure that you plant the alpines at the same depth as they were originally planted.

3 To improve the appearance of the planted trough, sprinkle stone chippings or fine gravel over the compost.

RIGHT A sink garden often looks better if you add a few small rocks among the alpines.

PLANTING A BARREL

1 Half-barrels are useful for large plants or for climbers that need a cane support, such as clematis on a wigwam of canes. You could also grow sweet peas, but use more than the three canes shown in step 3. Use a loam-based compost.

2 Plant three clematis (or other suitable climbers) at a slight inward angle.

3 Insert three canes so they cross at the top. Tie them together with garden twine, or use a proprietary cane holder.

4 Tie the plants to the canes. Eventually they may reach the top of the canes and begin to tumble down and become almost self-supporting.

TREES AND SHRUBS IN TUBS

Give your patio a touch of distinction by growing a few trees and shrubs in large tubs or pots. They are a lot less trouble to look after than seasonal plants, and many look attractive all year round.

PLANTING A TREE

1 RIGHT Always choose a large container – at least 30cm (12in) in diameter. If choosing an ornamental ceramic pot, make sure that it is frostproof. Always insert the usual drainage layer at the bottom before adding the compost. Fill with enough compost to bring the top of the root ball 2.5–5cm (1–2in) below the rim of the container. Be sure to use a loam-based compost, which has the weight and stability to support a tree in windy weather.

2 LEFT Remove the tree from its container and stand it on the new compost. Trickle more compost around the sides.

3 A tree will offer a lot of wind resistance, so ram the compost firmly around the root ball to ensure stability.

PLANTING SHRUBS

1 You can plant single specimen shrubs – such as a camellia, rhododendron, or *Choisya ternata* 'Sundance' – but a collection of dwarf shrubs with contrasting or colourful foliage is often more attractive for a longer period. Stand the plants in a group first to make sure they look good when positioned together.

2 Knock the plants out of their pots and plant firmly, making sure they are at their original depth in the soil or compost.

3 Add a finishing touch by covering the visible surface of the soil or compost with a mulch of gravel, cocoa shells or expanded clay granules.

RIGHT A group of small shrubs can be as effective as one large specimen. Here, a hebe, dwarf euonymus and *Santolina chamaecyparissus* have been planted as a group.

TREES IN TUBS

If the base of the tree looks bare, plant it with shade-tolerant plants such as ivies, plant some spring bulbs, or sow some quick and easy hardy annuals for added interest while the tree is becoming established.

A SUITABLE COMPOST

Use a loam-based compost for trees and shrubs. If you are growing a shrub that dislikes lime in the soil, such as a camellia or rhododendron, buy a compost described as an ericaceous mix. This will be more acid than other types of compost.

Caring For Plants In Containers

If you look after your plants in containers they will reward you with healthy growth and a good show. If you neglect basic care like feeding and watering, however, the results are sure to be disappointing. This is an area of gardening where the benefits of care and attention can be seen and enjoyed.

FEEDING YOUR PLANTS

1 If you can't remember to feed regularly, try placing a sachet of slow-release fertilizer beneath each plant. This releases its nutrients slowly over a period of months.

2 Instead of using sachets you can add a slow-release or controlled-release fertilizer to the compost. The latter only releases its nutrients when the weather is warm enough for the plants to benefit from it.

WATERING YOUR PLANTS

1 An automatic watering system is ideal for a group of containers close together on a patio. Run a small drip tube from the main supply pipe into each container, and adjust the flow rate if necessary to suit the size of the container.

2 If you have a lot of containers to water, a hosepipe is the most practical solution. Fit an outside tap, and if necessary run permanent piping to various parts of the garden so that you can attach a short length of hose with a push-on fitting wherever needed.

3 Use a lance attachment fitted to a hose, compression sprayer, or special basket pump to water hanging baskets.

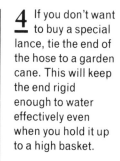

4 If you don't want to buy a special lance, tie the end of the hose to a garden cane. This will keep the end rigid enough to water effectively even when you hold it up to a high basket.

3 Soluble and liquid fertilizers are quick-acting and usually produce rapid results, but are more of a chore to apply. Feed regularly at the rate and frequency recommended by the manufacturer for best results.

4 Remember to feed trees and shrubs, as the compost has to sustain a lot of growth over a long period. Sprinkle a slow-release or controlled-release fertilizer over the surface in spring, and if possible fork it into the top 2.5cm (1in) or more of compost.

ROUTINE CARE

1 Many summer bedding plants cease flowering early if you allow the flowers to set seed. The plants often look tidier if dead-headed, and many will continue to flower for longer. Do not attempt to dead-head plants with masses of small flowers, such as lobelia, but you should be able to keep anything large, such as a pansy, dead-headed without difficulty.

2 Give summer bedding plants a health check at least once a week. Remove any yellowing leaves before they start to rot or mar the overall effect. Also remove any leaves that are showing signs of pests or diseases unless you know you can control them with sprays.

3 Control pests and diseases as you would elsewhere in the garden. Prompt action is especially important for plants in containers as they are usually planted very close together and the problem can spread quickly. Systemic insecticides and fungicides are the most effective, as it is difficult to achieve complete cover with a contact spray among such dense growth.

MAKING A POND

Old-fashioned concrete ponds used to be difficult to construct, but with modern liners and pre-formed pools, making a pond is a job you can complete in a weekend.

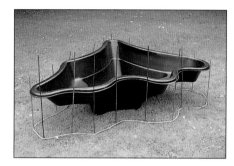

1 Place the pre-formed pool on level ground, then insert canes around the edge and lay a piece of rope around them to transfer the outline to the ground.

2 Excavate the hole, following the profile of the pond and its shelves, as accurately as you can. It will be necessary to take measurements and to lay the pond in the hole from time to time to check the fit. Do not be afraid to make the hole a few centimetres (inches) larger all around than the actual pond, as this will make backfilling easier later.

3 If you need to check that the depth is correct, lay a piece of wood across the excavation, making sure it is level, then measure down from this. If the soil is very stony, excavate an extra 5cm (2in) and line it with that depth of sand.

4 Place the pool in the excavation and check that it is absolutely level in all directions.

5 Run water into the pond and, as the level rises, pack fine soil around the edge. If you synchronize the filling with the packing, you are unlikely to disturb the levels.

6 Be sure to pack soil firmly beneath the shelves to avoid causing stresses within the moulding. Use a piece of wood to ram the soil into place if necessary. The backfilling may push the pool upwards, so check the level frequently as you fill and pack.

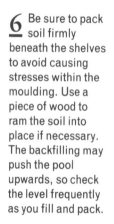

MARGINAL SHELVES

Although most waterlilies prefer the deeper water in the centre of the pool, the majority of aquatic plants grow in shallow water. A marginal shelf will enable you to grow many kinds of plants.

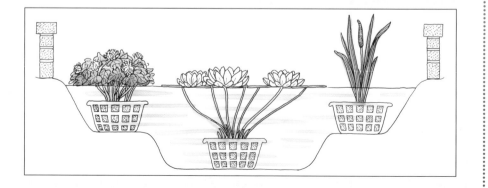

A LINER POND

1 Mark out the shape of your pond, using a length of rope or a hosepipe. If doing the job in winter, run some hot water through the hose first to make it supple.

2 Dig out the soil to the required depth and barrow it away unless you want to make a raised rock garden behind the pond. Leave a shallow ledge about 23cm (9in) wide about half-way down the total depth of the pool. Remove grass from around the edge to allow for the paving which will be used to produce a neat edge. Make this shelf deep enough for the thickness of the paving plus a bed of mortar.

3 Make sure the edge of the pond is level. Space short wooden pegs 90cm–1.2m (3–4ft) apart around the edge of the pool, and go around the pool with a spirit-level.

4 Make sure there are no sharp stones or thick roots sticking out of the soil, then place a cushion of about 12mm (½in) of sand on the bottom and the marginal shelves – also on the sides if possible (if you slope the sides slightly and use damp sand it should adhere). If the soil is very stony, use a polyester mat instead of sand. You can buy special matting designed for the job from water garden specialists.

5 Drape the liner loosely in the excavation, making sure that there is sufficient overlap all around. Hold the edges in place with a few bricks. Run in water from a hosepipe.

6 Lift the bricks from around the edge and allow the liner to move a little from time to time as the pond fills up with water. There will inevitably be some creases. Remove the worst of them by stretching and adjusting the liner as it fills.

7 Once the pond has been filled to its final level, cut off the surplus liner, leaving a flap of about 15cm (6in) all the way round. This will be covered and held in place by the mortar and paving.

8 Bed a paved edge on a mortar bed of three parts sand to one part cement. Rectangular paving slabs are the easiest to use for a rectangular pond, but use crazy-paving for an irregular shape such as this.

Stocking The Pond

The best time to stock the pond with plants is between mid spring and early summer. Do not put any tender floating aquatics into the pond until there is no risk of frost. Add fish at any time, but it is best to wait for a few weeks if the pond is new and only recently planted.

Planting A Waterlily

1 Although you can plant waterlilies and other deep-water plants in special planting baskets, an old washing-up bowl holds more compost and has room for expansion. Fill it with soil or an aquatic compost and plant the lily in this.

2 Always add oxygenating plants. If you use a washing-up bowl, plant some of these around the edge, otherwise plant in their own containers. Many oxygenators lack a developed root system, so just push the ends into the soil.

3 Cover the surface of the compost with gravel. This will help to anchor the plants down and prevent them floating out before they have rooted. It will also reduce the likelihood of fish making the water cloudy by stirring up the mud.

4 If it is early in the season and the waterlilies have not yet grown long stems, place the container on a few bricks or blocks. When the leaf stems have grown longer, remove the bricks so that the container sits on the bottom of the pond.

FLOWERS & FOLIAGE

PLANTING MARGINAL AQUATICS

1 Buy a special planting basket, and line it with turf or hessian, or a special basket liner, to hold in the compost.

2 Remove the plant from its pot and place it in the container. If the plant is small, put soil or compost at the bottom. Add garden soil or aquatic compost, not soil recently enriched with manure or fertilizer.

3 Cover with gravel to help anchor the plant and reduce the amount of soil or compost released into the pond when you submerge the basket.

4 Gently lower the basket into the water so that it sits on one of the marginal shelves. Make sure that the top of the basket is covered with water.

ADDING FISH

2 After a couple of hours, release the fish by opening the bag and letting it or them swim free. Do not leave the fish in the bag longer than necessary as they may begin to be starved of oxygen.

1 Never release fish directly into the pond when you get them home. Float the bag on the surface for a couple of hours so that the temperature of the water in the bag and the pond equalize.

FLOATING PLANTS

Some aquatics don't need planting. Floaters like water lettuce only need placing on the surface.

POND MAINTENANCE

Ponds do not need a lot of maintenance, but you should spend a couple of hours in the spring and autumn to keep the water sparkling and the plants attractive. Should you stock fish, be prepared to keep a small area of water free of ice if there is a prolonged freeze during the winter.

CLEANING THE POND

1 After two or three years your pond will probably benefit from a thorough clean. If possible, use the pond pump to empty most of the water, but do not let the water drop below the level of the pump otherwise it may be damaged. Finish emptying the pond with a bucket.

2 The fish will be easier to catch once the water level is low. Keep them in containers filled with the old pond water. Cover with netting to prevent them jumping out.

3 Remove all the plants, scrub off the worst of the dirt and mud, then rinse with a hose. Scoop out the dirty water with a bucket.

4 Refill with tap water. This contains chlorine, which is harmful to fish, so if possible keep the fish in their temporary homes for a few days before returning them to the pond.

5 Take the opportunity to divide and repot overcrowded plants.

6 Pull or cut each plant apart to make several smaller pieces.

7 Repot each portion individually. Remember to cover the surface of the compost/planting medium/pot with gravel before replacing in the pond.

FLOWERS & FOLIAGE

158

SPRING AND SUMMER POND CARE

1 Algae that turn the water green in the spring and early summer will usually disappear once the large plants are growing well, absorbing the nutrients and shading the water. But if you find it difficult to control, water in one of the chemical controls available. Follow the manufacturer's instructions and application rates very carefully.

2 Reduce blanket weed, which looks rather like green cotton wool, by twisting it around a cane or stick. This filamentous alga can also be controlled with an algicide, but mechanical measures like this may be enough to keep it in check.

AUTUMN POND CARE

1 Rake out as many leaves as possible before they sink and start to rot. A lawn rake is ideal for this, and you may be able to rake out many leaves that have already sunk to the bottom – but be careful with the rake if your pond is made with a liner.

3 Trim off dying leaves from marginal plants or those around the edge of the pond that are overhanging the side. Reduce the amount of vegetation that may rot in the pond during the winter.

2 If submerged oxygenating plants, such as elodea, or rampant growers like myriophyllum, have become overgrown, rake some of them out.

4 To prevent more leaves falling in, cover the pond with netting if possible. Peg it into position around the edge. A mesh like this will catch most leaves, which you should clear off periodically. Remove the netting once leaf-fall is over.

WINTER POND CARE

1 Should you have fish, float tennis or other balls on the surface if a severe frost is forecast. If the pond freezes over, you can tap the balls gently to provide small areas free of ice. The water will soon refreeze, however, and this method is suitable only for short cold spells.

2 To release toxic gasses that may have built up in a pond that has been frozen for many days, stand a pan of hot water on the ice. Tie a string to the handle so that you can retrieve it if it sinks.

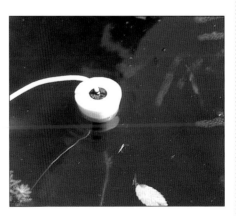

3 The best way to keep an area of pond ice-free is to use a pond heater. It costs no more than a large light bulb to run, and does the job very efficiently. There are mains and low-voltage versions.

GREENHOUSE BASICS

A basic greenhouse is simply a protective shell which you need to equip to display the plants effectively and to provide extra growing space. Adding an automatic ventilator opener should be regarded as an essential and not an optional extra.

INSTALLING AN AUTOMATIC VENTILATOR

1 Automatic ventilators are quick and easy to install. The method may vary with products from different manufacturers, so always follow their detailed instructions. This automatic ventilator is first fixed to the centre of the manual ventilator.

2 The other end of the bracket is bolted to the frame.

HIGH VENTILATORS

If you buy a large greenhouse where the manual ventilator is very difficult to reach, make sure that an easy-reach winder is also supplied.

3 Finally, the opener will need adjusting so that it opens and closes at the required temperatures.

Fixing A Shelf

1 Shelves are invaluable as they provide extra growing space. Those for aluminium greenhouses come in simple kits that you assemble yourself. Detailed assembly will vary according to make, but they should come with brackets that bolt together and fix into the mouldings of the aluminium greenhouse frame.

2 Assemble all the brackets for the shelves first, and use a spirit-level to check that they are all level.

3 Bolt the shelf to the bracket, using the nuts and bolts provided.

4 Some are available with end pieces to make a better-looking finish and reduce the dangers from hard metal corners.

Assembling An Integrated Bench

1 Fitted benches come with most metal greenhouses as an optional extra. They are worth buying as they will be designed to suit the size of the greenhouse. Follow the individual manufacturer's instructions, but they will almost certainly bolt to the greenhouse frame, with a surface that is also easily bolted together.

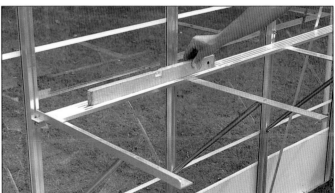

2 As soon as you have a length of surface in position, check the level. If it is not level, make adjustments at this stage, then finish assembling the surface.

GETTING THE BEST FROM YOUR GREENHOUSE

The greenhouse can be used to propagate many garden plants, as well as for crops such as tomatoes and cucumbers, and displays of flowering and foliage plants.

In winter you need to insulate your greenhouse to keep it warm; in summer you'll need to ventilate and shade it to keep it cool.

THERMAL SCREENS

A thermal screen made of polythene or a special fabric sold for the job will conserve heat if you pull it across at night. Suspend it on wires that run along the eaves. Just push it to one end in the mornings, and pull it across the greenhouse in the evenings.

If you want to reduce costs by heating just part of the greenhouse, separate it vertically with plastic sheeting. You may be able to buy a special kit; otherwise improvise by using fittings available from garden centres.

INSULATING A GREENHOUSE

1 If you have a metal-framed greenhouse, buy proprietary clips that fit into the moulding of the glazing bars. Designs vary, but with most you insert the clips first, then hold the polythene insulation in place by snapping on or pushing in a cap. If necessary, use adhesive tape to seal the overlaps and improve insulation.

2 If you have a timber-framed greenhouse, pin the insulation to the glazing bars with drawing pins or use proprietary suction fittings. It may be necessary to moisten the base of suction clips to get them to hold firmly to the glass.

3 Always insulate the ventilators separately so that they can be opened. It is important to ventilate an insulated greenhouse whenever practical to avoid diseases caused by high humidity.

SHADING A GREENHOUSE

1 A paint-on shading wash is a cheap and easy way to reduce the heating and scorching effect of the summer sun. Some become more transparent when wet, increasing the light on a dull day. Shading washes are easy to apply with a paintbrush.

2 You can save time if the greenhouse is large by applying the shading wash with a sprayer. But try to avoid the spray drifting over the surrounding glazing bars.

3 At the end of summer, simply remove the shading with a cloth or duster when it's dry. Although it does not wash off in the rain, it is easy to rub off when dry.

4 Internal shading is less effective than external because the temperature inside the greenhouse has already been raised by the effect of the sun on the glass, but it's better than no shading. Fix a plastic net sold for greenhouse shading to the inside of the glazing bars, using the type of clips used for insulation.

EXTERIOR ROLLER BLINDS

External roller blinds are very effective, and much more flexible than a shading wash because you can remove or apply the shading to suit the daily weather.

HOW TO MAKE A CAPILLARY BENCH

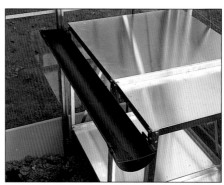

1 To make a capillary bench from metal or wooden staging, first fix a length of plastic gutter to the edge (you may have to use gutter brackets) and lay a sheet of polythene over the bench.

2 Cut a length of capillary matting (available from garden centres) to size, leaving one edge long to fold over into the gutter. Keep the gutter topped up with water by hand or with a length of tubing coupled to a constant-level valve.

WATERING THE GREENHOUSE

FLOWERS & FOLIAGE

Watering is the most demanding aspect of greenhouse gardening – it is a daily chore for much of the year. But you can make life easier for yourself with an automatic watering system.

INSTALLING A CAPILLARY BENCH

Lay capillary matting (available from garden centres and shops) over the whole bench. Cut the matting to size, and do not leave any trailing over the edge of the bench, otherwise it may drain the water away.

You can devise your own constant-level reservoir using a ball valve, but it is easier to buy one designed for the job which can be connected to the mains. If you do not have a convenient mains supply buy one designed for use with a bag (the hose connector will be a different size).

Use a piece of capillary matting as a wick to draw water from the reservoir to the bench matting.

HAND-WATERING

1 If you find it difficult to judge moisture visually in a pot, especially if it contains a peat-based compost, press your finger into the surface.

2 Alternatively, use moisture indicators in a few representative pots.

OVERHEAD SPRAYING

If you prefer a system that waters your greenhouse with a spray, buy one that you can suspend from the roof. Designs vary, but usually you can screw nozzles into the tubing at intervals. Some are designed to spray water on both sides of the greenhouse, others are for spraying just one side.

IMPROVISING

Although you can buy capillary watering systems with special reservoirs, you can easily improvise. This system uses a length of plastic gutter as a reservoir, into which one end of the capillary mat is inserted.

Keep the gutter topped up with water by hand, from a cistern, or dip fed by a water bag.

BOTTOM PICTURE Although capillary benches are useful for established plants, seedlings and cuttings that have not yet made a good root system are usually best watered by hand or an automatic overhead watering system.

3 Established plants in large pots are best watered without a rose on the can. Use a finger over the end to break the force of the water . . . or stuff a small piece of rag into the end to reduce the flow.

4 Water seedlings with a rose on the can. While the seedlings are small, use the can with the rose facing upwards so that the water falls more gently.

FLOWERS & FOLIAGE

165

DISPLAYING AND CARING FOR GREENHOUSE PLANTS

Keep your greenhouse looking good by arranging your pot plants attractively. Remember to feed as well as water them, and keep the atmosphere good for growing.

MAKE THE MOST OF SHELVES

Shelves are useful for trays of seedlings in spring, when staging is never sufficient. You can also use them to display pot plants during the summer. Use plenty of trailers, but make sure that you do not shade the plants beneath too much.

HANGING SHELVES

Some shelves are designed to be suspended from the roof glazing bars. Others are fixed by brackets to the glazing bars of the sides or end of the greenhouse. Choose an appropriate type.

POT PLANTS

If you have lots of large pot plants, try growing a collection of them in the greenhouse border instead of on shelving. Just plunge the pots into the border soil or plant directly into the soil.

STAGING DISPLAYS

1 Build up your display to different heights to make the most of available space and to create a more spectacular show. To raise the height of plants at the back, stand them on inverted empty pots . . . and use trailers at the front to cascade over the edge.

2 Tiered proprietary staging is useful for making the most of available space. Use the bottom shelves for resting plants that do not need much light, or to store pots and trays.

3 Large self-watering containers are intended for use indoors, but use them in your greenhouse to create an eye-catching display, perhaps at the end of the path. Plant up a large tub with a collection of bold feature plants that look good together or just one striking plant such as this aubergine.

Although this is a larger greenhouse than you are likely to have in your garden, the same kind of display can be achieved on a more modest scale.

CLIMBERS

If you have a lean-to greenhouse, paint the back wall white to reflect light and to act as an attractive background for wall shrubs and climbers. Plant greenhouse climbers in the border and train them against wires fixed to the back wall.

CREATING THE RIGHT ATMOSPHERE

1 Always fit at least one automatic ventilator so that the temperature never becomes too high before you are around to open the windows. Open more ventilators – or the door – to keep the greenhouse cool on a hot day.

2 Plants grow best in a humid atmosphere. Standing the pots on capillary matting or trays of moist gravel will help, but when the temperature is hot, damp down the greenhouse to create a more humid atmosphere. Splash water over the paths, using a watering-can.

COLD FRAMES

Cold frames are invaluable for overwintering vulnerable plants if you don't have a greenhouse. And if you do, they will be invaluable as an 'overflow' in late spring and for hardening off (acclimatizing) seedlings before you plant them out. To get the best from your frame, insulate it against severe frosts.

ERECTING A COLD FRAME FROM A KIT

1 Aluminium-framed cold frames are much easier to construct than the old-fashioned brick-walled type, and they come in kit form with all that you will need, including glass. Check that you have all the components for the frame when you open the box.

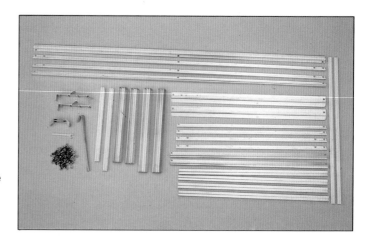

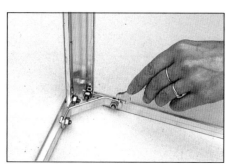

2 Bolt the frame together in the order suggested by the manufacturer.

3 When the main frame has been bolted together, insert the glass. It will be held in place with clips or glazing strips according to the design. Slide on or fix the 'lights' (hinged tops) as instructed. Make sure that they lift or slide easily.

INSULATING A COLD FRAME

1 A glass and aluminium cold frame will be much colder than a brick-walled one. If you want to offer your plants more protection in winter, insulate the sides and ends with expanded polystyrene. Cut the expanded polystyrene to fit the end of the frame first. If necessary, make a template from paper or cardboard.

2 Cut the side pieces, bearing in mind that you will have to allow for the thickness of the expanded polystyrene at each end. Push them into place. If you have cut them accurately, they should be a tight fit. If they are too loose, however, use small pieces of card wedged in at one end to hold them in position.

TYPES OF COLD FRAME

Aluminium frames are widely available in kit form and quick and easy to construct. They are usually glazed to the ground, so letting in more light. The drawback is that they quickly lose heat through the glazed sides unless you insulate them in the winter.

Wooden frames can also be bought as kits, but they are usually more expensive and are less widely available. You might be able to make your own. Many gardeners consider them attractive because they tend to blend in with the garden better than metal frames.

Brick-walled frames are seldom used by amateurs as their construction is more difficult and demands more skill. However, they generally protect the plants within much better than thin-walled frames.

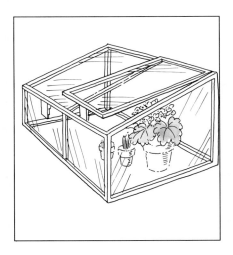

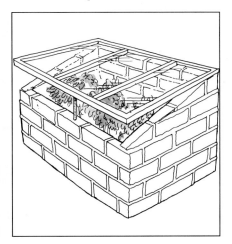

INSULATION AND VENTILATION

1 Never insulate the top of a frame permanently, unless using bubble polythene, because the plants need as much light as possible. When very cold nights are forecast give extra protection by covering the top with old carpet or other warm material. Put it in place before the temperature drops, and take it off in the morning unless the day is very cold.

2 Good ventilation is essential in warm weather, and useful even in the winter. Some frames have sliding tops, which are less prone to wind damage than lifting tops.

3 Lifting tops sometimes have an adjustable opening device, but if not you can make a simple wedge from a piece of wood. Cut a couple of notches in it so that you can open the top by different amounts as the plants are gradually hardened off.

FRUIT &
VEGETABLES

The kitchen garden holds its own special charm; a bed of plump onions ripening on the soil, clusters of tomatoes catching the sun, and crisp rows of succulent salad crops like lettuces all look as good as they taste. Add a few decorative herbs such as sages, marjorams and borage, and perhaps a few decorative espalier or cordon fruits, and you have a part of the garden that will compare well with the ornamental area.

OPPOSITE
The produce of the kitchen garden can look good as well as taste good. Apples like these 'Sunset' look particularly appetizing.

INTRODUCTION

Fruit, vegetables and herbs are particularly rewarding to grow. You can enjoy the results of your labours on your dinner plate, and many gardeners find neat rows of healthy vegetables or trained fruit trees laden with a heavy crop aesthetically pleasing too. Certainly, many herbs are highly ornamental and would be worth growing in the flower garden even if they had no culinary use.

The kitchen garden is particularly labour-intensive, however, and the difference between a mediocre and bumper crop can usually be accounted for by the amount of care and attention the plants receive. Many of the tips and techniques suggested in the following pages will help you to achieve better or bigger crops, and will help you to extend the harvesting seasons.

An early start can produce crops weeks ahead of the normal time, which means tasty home-grown produce earlier and at a time when it is more expensive in the shops. Cloches and the newer methods using floating cloches and horticultural fleece are among the

ABOVE Marrows and courgettes needs quite a lot of space, but even a single plant will yield a useful crop.

LEFT This pear 'Doyenne du Comice' is grown as a tree, but if you do not have space for a tree, grow one trained as a cordon or espalier.

techniques described and there are useful hints for extending the season into late autumn, plus lots of ideas for storing what you can't eat fresh.

There are also some helpful tips for bonus crops throughout the year – extra crops you can often encourage once the main harvest has been reaped.

Growing vegetables can be fun too, and even though you won't keep a family fed from a few windowboxes or containers on the patio, it is rewarding to harvest some early potatoes from a growing bag or pick pretty red-leaved cut-and-come-again lettuces from a windowbox. You will find plenty of

Although really huge onions for the show bench need a lot of care and attention, a crop like this is easy to grow from sets. Grow plenty of them to store for winter use.

ideas for growing a wide range of vegetables and herbs in containers in the greenhouse and outdoors.

Fruit trees are not only for gardeners with space for an orchard. You can grow fence- or wall-trained cordon or fan fruits even in a tiny garden, and there are columnar apple trees that take up hardly any space and look pretty too. The fruit section tells you how to get the best from your fruit, whatever the size of your garden.

To avoid repeated descriptions of routine tasks such as sowing, thinning, feeding and picking, the key cultivation tasks are summarized for vegetables and for fruit in extensive tables.

GROWING VEGETABLES AND HERBS

Make your kitchen garden as attractive and productive as possible through careful planning. And if space is limited, try growing some of the more decorative vegetables and herbs in flower beds.

CHOOSING A SITE

Almost all vegetables and most fruits require a sunny position to do well. Place fruit trees where they will not cast shade over the vegetables. Make sure that herbs are in the sunniest place unless planting one of the few varieties that prefer shade.

There's always space to grow a few herbs. Many make attractive container plants.

DISPLAYING HERBS

Many herbs are leafy and rather dull, and a formal herb garden is a good way to display them. If it has a strong geometric shape it will be a feature even in the winter when most herbs have died down. If you have the space, make it complex and ornate, with formal paths dividing the beds, and perhaps an ornament such as a birdbath or sundial as a centrepiece.

If you do not have space for a formal herb garden, a 'chequer-board' herb garden created by lifting alternate and staggered

paving stones makes an interesting feature for a large patio.

Most herbs do well in containers, and the compact ornamental herbs such as thymes and marjorams are particularly ideal.

Many herbs are decorative enough to grow in the flower border. Place tall ones such as fennel and lovage at the back among herbaceous border plants, low-growing ones such as chives and golden marjoram as an edging.

WAYS WITH VEGETABLES

The conventional method of growing vegetables is in long rows.

ABOVE A basketful of courgettes is just one of the regular delights in store for anyone willing to find space for a few vegetables.

OPPOSITE The kitchen garden can look quite attractive as well as being productive. The 1.2m (4ft) bed system has been used on this plot.

This is a convenient way to grow them, and if the rows are kept well weeded, a vegetable garden can look very attractive too.

The 1.2m (4ft) bed system is popular with organic gardeners and those who want to minimize digging. Beds 1.2m (4ft) across are wide enough for cultivation to be carried out easily from the paths on each side. This means that you do not have to walk on the soil which can compact it, and if the ground has been well prepared first and is regularly mulched with organic material, you should not have to dig. You may need to adjust the normal spacings for the plants as there is no need to leave room to walk between the rows.

A surprisingly large range of vegetables can be grown in containers – even crops like peas and potatoes.

Some vegetables, such as red lettuces, beetroot and rhubarb chard, are decorative enough to be grown among flowers, if you don't mind leaving gaps once you begin to harvest them.

GROUNDWORK

A vegetable plot normally needs digging over at least once a year, and deep digging is particularly beneficial for some crops. To get the best from your ground, spend some time thinking about crop rotation and planning what vegetables to grow where.

CATCH CROPS AND INTERCROPS

To make the best use of available space, grow quick-maturing crops between slower-growing ones. If you plant lettuces so they fill the ground between sweet corn plants, they will help to keep the ground free of weeds and should be ready for harvesting before the developing sweet corn casts too much shade. If you mix radish seed with parsnip seed, the quick germination and rapid growth of the radishes will enable you to crop them before the slower parsnips need all the space.

Catch cropping enables you to sneak in a quick crop in cleared ground. If you lift early potatoes, you might be able to fit in a crop of lettuces or radishes before you need the space for winter crops.

DOUBLE DIGGING

1 Start by digging out a trench 60cm (2ft) wide and barrowing soil to the other end of the plot. If the plot is wide enough you can divide it into two, working up one side and down the next – in which case barrow the soil to the end of the row where the last trench will be.

2 Fork over the bottom of the trench. Traditionally, manure or garden compost was dug in at the same time, but only deep-rooting plants benefit from it at this depth. It is better to incorporate the manure or compost at a level where more plants will benefit from it.

3 Spread a generous layer of manure or garden compost over the area just forked over.

4 Dig out the next trench 60cm (2ft) wide, throwing the soil forward to fill the excavation left by the previous one. Fill in the last trench with the soil which was taken from the first one and put on one side.

CROP ROTATION

By rotating the position of various types of crop you can reduce the risk of certain pests and diseases building up in the soil, and you can group together crops with similar needs in terms of soil fertility and its pH level.

There are several variations, and some people use a four-year rotation, but in a small garden or allotment the three-year rotation shown below would be more appropriate.

One part is kept for perennial crops, and the rest divided up into three parts. Each year the crops are rotated within these three areas as shown.

GROUP A

Grow: aubergines, beetroot, carrots, celeriac, celery, courgettes, cucumbers, garlic, leeks, marrows, onions, parsnips, peppers, potatoes, pumpkins, salsify, scorzonera, shallots, tomatoes.
Dig and feed: double dig, add manure, and feed crops during the growing season if necessary.

GROUP B

Grow: broad beans, chicory, endive, French beans, lettuce, peas, runner beans, spinach, Swiss chard, sweet corn.
Dig and feed: single dig, and apply a general garden fertilizer at the beginning of the season, before sowing or soon after growth starts.

GROUP C

Grow: broccoli, Brussels sprouts, cabbages, cauliflowers, kale, kohl rabi, turnips, radishes, swedes.
Dig and feed: single dig, add lime if necessary, to bring the soil to a pH of 6.5–7.0. Apply a general garden fertilizer in the spring, and supplement with additional fertilizer during the season if necessary.

GROUP D

Grow: any crops that need to remain in the same piece of ground undisturbed, such as asparagus, globe artichokes and rhubarb, or plants that can be left in place or lifted annually such as Jerusalem artichokes.

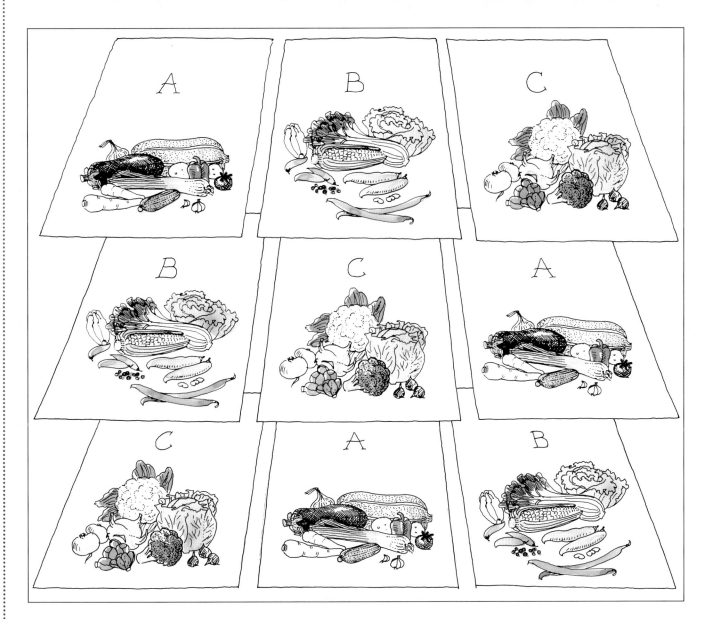

MANURES AND FERTILIZERS

Fruit and vegetables need plenty of feeding if you want good crops. Synthetic fertilizers are useful for a short-term boost, but by adding humus (and the nutrients contained in garden compost and animal manures) to the soil, you will be improving the soil structure as well as feeding the plants. This almost always leads to better crops than those grown using artificial fertilizers alone for many years.

ADDING FERTILIZERS

1 A fertilizer distributor is the quickest and most efficient way to apply fertilizer to an allotment or large kitchen garden. Once the distribution rate has been calculated, simply fill the hopper and push the distributor along in rows.

2 Measure out the amount of fertilizer required for a square metre or yard if applying by hand. If liked, pour the measured amount into a suitable container that you can discard afterwards, and make a note of how full it is. If necessary, make a mark at the appropriate level.

3 Mark off the area with strings stretched 1m (1yd) apart. Then use canes cut to 1m (1yd) to divide the area into metre or yard squares. When you have applied fertilizer to one square, pick up the redundant cane and place it 1m (1yd) further along.

4 Pour the fertilizer into your free hand then scatter it as evenly as possible over the area. For each square, use the small measure, previously marked at the correct level, to scoop up the right amount of fertilizer each time.

5 Rake the fertilizer into the surface before sowing or planting.

6 Some plants need a boost while they are growing. Cabbages often benefit from a dose of a nitrogenous fertilizer such as sulphate of ammonia. Sprinkle it around the individual plants, no further out than the spread of the foliage, but be careful to keep it off the leaves and stems. Hoe or water it in afterwards.

7 Most fruit trees will benefit from a general garden fertilizer applied in the spring. Sprinkle it around the base of the tree, keeping it off the trunk, then hoe it in.

MAKING GARDEN COMPOST

1 Compost bins – home-made or bought – are useful and often aesthetically more pleasing than an exposed compost heap, but in the kitchen garden you can save money by making an ordinary heap like this. Start with a thick layer of waste vegetable material. Make the heap at least 1m (1yd) square, and preferably larger.

2 Tread the heap to compact the material when it is about 30cm (1ft) deep. Then add a sprinkling of sulphate of ammonia or a commercial compost accelerator.

3 Continue to add garden and kitchen waste, along with grass cuttings (but not if you have recently used a weedkiller on the lawn).

4 Continue to build up the heap in layers like this, and if possible water the heap whenever the weather is very dry.

5 After several months, depending on the time of year and the weather, the compost will be ready for use. Use any unrotted compost from around the edges to form the base for a new heap.

An Early Start 1

Cloches are the next best thing to a greenhouse or cold frame, and are indispensable if you want to enjoy your own fresh vegetables early or late in the season when they are more expensive in the shops.

Warming the Soil

1 In spring, put the cloches in place a couple of weeks before sowing or planting, to warm up the ground.

2 Pay attention to the end pieces, otherwise the cloche will become a wind tunnel and not retain the heat. With simple cloches these ends may just be a sheet of glass, but proprietary cloches may have specially designed ends. Always make sure the cloche is secure – a couple of strong pegs pushed into the ground are usually sufficient anchorage.

3 **RIGHT** Plant out early vegetables that are hardy, such as broad (fava) beans, or the hardiest varieties of crops like lettuces, once the ground has had a week or two to warm up. Make as much use as possible of the space in a large cloche. For example, sow a row of radishes or carrots either side of the lettuces.

4 **RIGHT** Tent cloches are less expensive than the barn cloches, but are just as good for warming up the ground and offering early protection for seedlings. Once the seedlings become too large, move the cloches to a new position to germinate later seedlings.

Tunnel Cloches

1 Plastic tunnel cloches are useful for starting off early vegetable seedlings. Put them in place a week or two before you sow, to give the soil time to warm up.

2 Make sure the plastic is held firmly by the securing wires, otherwise strong winds will damage the cloche.

3 Secure both ends firmly to resist the wind, and make sure the plastic is pulled taut.

FLEECY FILMS

1 Horticultural fleece will protect your crops from a degree or two of frost, and will deter many pests too. Once the seeds have been sown, pull the fleece over the area, holding it down with a few bricks or large stones.

2 Lay the fleece loosely over the area, so there is some movement that will allow the crops to grow, but cover the edges with soil to ensure that no large gaps are left. Water the plants normally.

WHEN TO USE FLOATING CLOCHES

Floating cloches are generally used in the spring, but they can be useful for autumn protection too. Liquids will penetrate them, so you can water and apply liquid feeds through them. To weed or feed with non-liquid fertilizer, peel back the material and replace it when you have finished.

Many vegetables can be left under the cloche until they mature, but do not keep covered any plants that need pollinating, such as dwarf beans.

FLOATING CLOCHES

Protective netting floating cloches give some protection against wind and hail, and exclude many pests. And they provide a little frost protection. Peel back the netting if you need to weed or thin the plants, and replace it in position afterwards.

Perforated plastic film (right) will protect seedlings like other floating cloches. It is likely to be cheaper but not as long-lasting.

4 Use soil to hold down the edges of the cloche, to reduce the risk of the wind lifting the sides.

5 Pull up the side of the cloche and use a soil thermometer to check that the soil has warmed up enough for germination. Most vegetables will germinate only if the soil temperature is above 7°C (45°F).

6 Either remove the cloche for sowing or planting, or pull the plastic up on one side of the cloche.

AN EARLY START 2

Many vegetables can be started off in pots or seed trays so that they are already growing well when you plant them out. You will be able to harvest them many weeks before those sown in the open ground.

RIGHT Cabbages can be sown outdoors, but for an early start they can be sown indoors and raised on pots.

STARTING OFF SHALLOTS AND GARLIC

1 Start off large shallots in pots in a greenhouse or cold frame, in early or mid winter. Plant so that the base of the bulb just sits in the compost. Use a loam-based compost or garden soil.

2 Place the pots in a cold frame or greenhouse, and keep moist but not wet. The crops will grow better in gentle warmth, but they do not need much heat. Try to keep them growing slowly and in a good light. Plant them in the garden, about 15–20cm (6–8in) apart, in early spring.

3 Garlic is best planted in the garden in the autumn rather than the spring. If you missed the opportunity then, start them off in pots like shallots (left) or put them into modules like these in mid or late winter, covering them with about 2.5cm (1in) of compost. Plant out 10–15cm (4–6in) apart in early spring.

AN EARLY ROW OF PEAS

1 Sow an early variety of peas in a length of plastic guttering filled with good garden soil. Stagger the peas in two rows as shown. Cover them with more soil, then keep in the greenhouse until the seedlings are about 8cm (3in) tall. Make sure they are in good light.

2 Dig a wide drill the depth of the guttering, using a draw hoe. If liked, use a garden line to make sure you keep the drill in a straight line.

3 Slide the compost containing the pea seedlings out of the length of gutter and into the drill. Firm the soil around the new row of peas, then cover with cloches to advance growth even further.

FRUIT & VEGETABLES

EARLY RUNNER BEANS

1 About six to eight weeks before the last frost is likely, sow some runner bean seeds in 15–20cm (6–8in) pots. Place three seeds in each pot – if they all germinate you can thin to two plants in each pot.

2 Cover the seeds with about 5cm (2in) of compost. Place the pots in a light position in a frost-free greenhouse, and keep the seedlings well watered.

3 About a fortnight before you want to plant them out, harden them off in a cold frame. Protect against frost. Plant out when it is safe to do so.

SOWING IN POTS

1 Many vegetables can be given a good start if they are sown in pots, and it is a particularly useful method for brassicas (members of the cabbage family) if you have club-root disease in the soil. The plants will have a good start and be more able to resist the disease, provided you use a good sterilized compost. Sow about three seeds in each pot.

2 If more than one seed germinates, thin to leave just one seedling in each pot.

3 After hardening off (acclimatizing) the seedlings in a cold frame, knock them out of their pots and plant in the garden.

SOWING IN MODULES

1 Modules like this are useful for many types of vegetable seedlings, such as lettuce, that are planted out while still small and do not need a large amount of compost or space. Sow a couple of seeds in each.

2 If more than one seed germinates in a compartment, thin to one seedling while still small.

3 Make sure the seedlings have been watered before planting out, and remove each one with its root ball intact. Planted like this they will grow away quickly with the minimum check.

EXTENDING THE SEASON

Use your cloches at the end of the season as well as the beginning, and protect vegetables for winter use.

WINTER PROTECTION

RIGHT Some vegetables and herbs, such as parsley, will continue to crop for much longer if you cover the row with cloches before the cold weather arrives. Be sure to place a piece of glass over each end, so that the cloche does not become a wind tunnel.

PROTECT FROM FROST

1 In mild areas both beetroot and celeriac can be left in the ground for winter use if the soil is well drained. Protect them from severe frosts with a layer of straw about 15cm (6in) deep.

2 Where winters are cold, lift the vegetables and store in moist sand in a frost-free place. Twist the tops off by hand before storing.

FRUIT & VEGETABLES

SOW WINTER SALADS

1 To extend the choice of fresh winter vegetables, sow winter radishes and corn salad (lamb's lettuce) in late summer and early autumn, for picking during the winter months.

2 You can sow them in the open, but they do better in a cold frame or if you cover them with a cloche.

3 Winter radishes are sown in late summer. Lift the roots in late autumn to store in damp sand in a shed or cellar.

RIPEN LATE TOMATOES

Use cloches to ripen outdoor tomatoes at the end of the season, before the frost damages them. Lay straw on the ground to protect the fruits, then remove the supports and allow the plants to lie on the straw.

Cover the row with cloches to speed the ripening of the last of the tomatoes. Large barn cloches are best for this.

CORN SALAD

Sow corn salad (lamb's lettuce) in late summer. Harvest the leaves, a few at a time as needed, throughout the winter.

ENCOURAGING FURTHER CROPPING

Even after harvesting, it may be possible to induce some vegetables to produce a bonus crop.

EXTRA SPRING GREENS

Leave the stump after harvesting early cabbages for spring greens. You should be able to stimulate an extra crop of leaves. Make a cross-shaped cut in the stalk with a sharp knife. After a few weeks a cluster of small new heads will have grown. Harvest these for a bonus crop of spring greens.

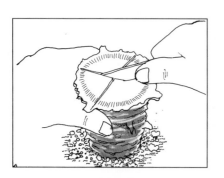

MORE CALABRESE

Cut the main head as normal, but do not discard the plant. Leave it to develop smaller heads on sideshoots.

After a few weeks, harvest the secondary heads that have developed on the sideshoots.

CUT-AND-COME-AGAIN LETTUCE

1 Loose-leaf lettuces such as 'Salad Bowl' can be harvested in stages. If you need just a few leaves, remove one or two leaves from several plants in the row.

2 If you need a whole head, try harvesting by cutting across the plant about 2.5cm (1in) above the soil. The stump should resprout for a second harvest.

HARVESTING SPINACH

1 You can harvest ordinary and New Zealand spinach a few leaves at a time, instead of uprooting whole plants. With New Zealand spinach harvest the tips of the stems as well as young leaves, to prevent flowering and encourage more side growths.

2 If you harvest whole plants of ordinary spinach, try cutting the leaves off 2.5cm (1in) above the ground. They will often regrow and produce another crop of leaves.

PAK CHOI AND CHINESE CABBAGES

Harvest some of your pak choi while they are still young. Cut off the leaves about 2.5cm (1in) above the soil. New leaves will usually be produced for a later crop.

Harvest Chinese cabbages by cutting them off about 2.5cm (1in) above the ground, to leave a stump. New growth will usually appear within weeks.

By growing a selection of different lettuce varieties, you will be able to harvest over a longer period . . . especially if you also stagger the sowings. Be sure to include some loose-leaf (oak-leaf) varieties that you can harvest as individual leaves, often over a period of several months.

187

SOWING VEGETABLES 1

Get your vegetables off to a good start by preparing the seed beds carefully, and if necessary use one of the special techniques described to get them going extra quickly.

PREPARING THE GROUND

1 Break down large clods of soil left after rough digging, to produce a fine surface for sowing.

2 Large lumps may be too difficult to break down with a rake or hand cultivator, especially if the soil is dry. Try treading on them to crumble them into smaller pieces.

3 Rake the soil level, gathering any large stones to one end.

4 Do not attempt to remove small stones, but any large ones are best gathered up and removed.

SOWING IN DRILLS

1 Always use a garden line to keep the rows straight. It is worth buying a proper garden line, which will last for years. Wind the surplus line tightly around the peg. Designs vary, but it should be possible to keep the line taut.

2 Use the corner of a hoe or rake to make the drill. Try to keep to the depth recommended on the seed packet.

3 Sprinkle the seeds thinly, to avoid unnecessary thinning later, and as evenly as possible. If you find this difficult, buy a proprietary seed dispenser designed to make this tricky chore easier.

Most gardeners sow their vegetables in long rows, but by using a 1.2m (4ft) bed system you can avoid having to tread on the ground to weed, cultivate and harvest, as you can easily reach the rows from the paths either side. Provided that you mulch heavily with garden compost or well-rotted manure, this can form the basis of a no-dig method of cultivation because the soil is not compacted.

The rows can be sown closer together with this method of cultivation.

4 If the soil is very dry, run water into the drill first to soak the soil. Water before sowing, because then there is less chance of the seeds being washed away.

5 Cover the seeds by shuffling your feet along the sides of the drill, knocking the excavated soil back into the drills.

6 You may find it easier to rake the soil back into the drill, but be careful to rake in the direction of the drill and not across it.

SOWING VEGETABLES 2

Although most vegetables are best sown in conventional single rows, some can be sown broadcast, and others are better if sown in multiple rows. Consider fluid sowing where you need to get tricky crops off to an early start.

Whether sowing broadcast or in drills (rows), closer spacing is possible if you grow your vegetables in 1.2m (4ft) beds because weeding and cultivation is carried out from either side. Traditional row spacings allow for having to walk between the plants for routine cultivation.

SOWING MULTIPLE ROWS

1 Some seeds, such as peas and French beans, are usually sown in multiple rows close together. Take out a wide drill with a draw hoe.

2 Space the seeds in the bottom of the drill. Large seeds like peas and beans can be spaced accurately by hand.

3 Pull the soil back into the drill with the draw hoe or a rake. If mice or birds are a problem in your area, try covering the drills with fine mesh wire-netting until the seeds germinate.

FLUID SOWING

1 Fluid sowing is a way of getting seeds off to a quick start outdoors. Use it for slow-germinating seeds such as parsnips and parsley, and to get early carrots and onions off to a flying start. Sow the seeds thickly on damp kitchen paper. Keep in a warm place, such as an airing cupboard.

2 Check the seeds daily, and make sure that they remain moist. Keeping them covered will help. As soon as the roots start to emerge (don't wait for the leaves to grow), wash them off the paper into a sieve.

3 Mix up some wallpaper paste (choose one without a fungicide), or buy a fluid sowing kit containing a special gel from your garden centre. Stir the seeds into the gel to distribute them thoroughly.

4 Take out the drill as you would normally, at the usual depth.

5 Place the paste in a plastic bag, and cut off one corner – rather like making an icing bag. Do not make the hole too large. Twist the top of the bag to prevent the paste oozing out, then move the bag along the drill as you press the paste out of the cut-off corner. Cover with soil in the usual way, and don't forget to water if the soil is dry.

SOWING BROADCAST

1 Some seeds, such as cereal and grass seeds, and especially those sown in a seed bed for transplanting later, such as cabbages, can be sown broadcast. Scatter as evenly as possible on prepared soil.

2 Rake the seeds into the soil. Rake in the opposite direction to that used when the ground was prepared for sowing. This helps to bury and distribute the seeds more effectively in the soil.

THINNING AND TRANSPLANTING

Thin your vegetables while they are still small, preferably in two stages so that you end up with a full row of well-spaced plants. Take special care, too, with those vegetables that may have to be transplanted, as this is a very vulnerable time for them.

MULTIPLE SOWING

Some growers plant out certain vegetables – such as leeks, onions, carrots and beetroot – in small clusters of seedlings.

They are best grown in modules, with perhaps four or six seeds in each cell.

Plant out intact and do not attempt to separate them. You will not get exhibition vegetables, but the overall weight of crop is often good.

BEWARE CARROT FLY

The carrot fly lays eggs around carrots when they are thinned. Thinning can leave the soil more open, and the smell of the crushed leaves is thought to attract it.

Thin in the evening, and nip the surplus plants off at ground level instead of pulling them up.

Take the thinnings away with you rather than leaving them on the ground.

THINNING

1 Thin as soon as the seedlings are large enough to handle conveniently, but leave the remaining seedlings twice as close as the final spacing. This will allow for losses while they are still young. If the seedlings are very close together, try pinching off surplus seedlings at soil level, to reduce disturbance to those left behind.

2 When the seedlings are almost touching, thin to their final spacing. If there are gaps it may be possible to lift some of the thinnings carefully and transplant them to make good the gaps.

TRANSPLANTING

1 When transplanting from open ground, water thoroughly an hour beforehand if the weather is dry.

2 Loosen the soil with a garden fork if there are a lot of closely spaced seedlings to transplant, otherwise lift them with a trowel or hand fork. If possible, lift each seedling individually with a ball of soil attached to the roots.

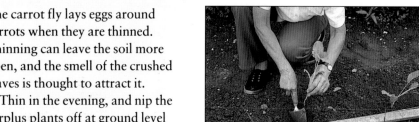

3 Plant with a trowel and firm the soil around the roots. To avoid having to firm with the hands, insert the blade of the trowel about 5cm (2in) away from the plant and press it firmly towards the roots.

4 You can firm the soil with the handle of the trowel instead, but if the soil is damp it will make the trowel dirty and unpleasant to use.

PLANTING OUT FROM MODULES, TRAYS AND POTS

1 Make sure the compost is moist before carefully removing the seedling from the module, tray or pot. To remove the seedling from a module, squeeze it out from the base while gently pulling at the top.

2 A plant grown in a pot will usually come out cleanly if you invert it, holding the plant between your fingers, and shake gently. If it does not come out readily, tap the bottom of the pot, or knock the rim against a hard surface.

3 Plant the seedlings with a trowel, at their final spacing, then firm the soil gently and water in well.

PLANTING BRASSICAS

1 If club-root is a problem, grow your brassica seedlings in pots of sterilized compost and plant them out when they are growing strongly. This will not eliminate the disease, but the plants get a good start and the effects are minimized.

2 Brassicas are also attacked by cabbage root fly, the larvae of which burrow into the roots and stems. Place a proprietary or improvised brassica collar around each seedling, making sure it lies flat on the soil. This will deter the flies from laying their eggs at the base of the plant.

STAKING AND SUPPORTING

Runner and climbing French beans, tall peas and even tomatoes need some form of support. Choose appropriate supports and insert them while the plants are still small.

GROWING BAG SUPPORTS

You can buy cane supports for growing bags, and this is just one type. They hold the canes in place even though the depth of compost in the bag is insufficient to hold them upright on their own. Although these add to the expense of the canes, they will last many seasons if you look after them carefully.

PEA STICKS

Save twiggy sticks from prunings, or cut them from a suitable tree. Use tall ones for tall varieties of peas, the smaller ones for dwarf varieties. Push the sticks into the ground between the peas when they are about 5cm (2in) high. The peas will support themselves by curling their tendrils round the sticks. Once the plants have finished cropping, pull them up and save the pea sticks for another year.

NETTING

Nylon netting is a good support for both peas and beans. Stretch it between two stout posts or make a framework of battens or canes. Use a 10cm (4in) mesh, and tie it on securely. Remember that the net will offer a lot of wind resistance when covered with foliage. You may have to thread young beans through to start them climbing.

Bamboo Canes

1 If you have just a few runner bean plants, grow them up a wigwam of canes. They will even look attractive at the back of a flower border if grown in this way. Tie about four to six canes together close to the top so they form a sort of wigwam. Alternatively, it is possible to buy a proprietary plastic holder through which you can push the canes.

2 Runner beans will twine around the canes and will be self-clinging once they start to grow in this way. Start them off by winding them round the canes initially, to keep the shoots off the soil, where they are more vulnerable to slug and snail damage.

3 For a whole row of runner beans or climbing French beans, insert two rows of 2.4m (8ft) canes at a slight angle so they cross near the top.

4 Slide a horizontal cane along the top in the V formed by the crossed canes. Pull it downwards so the canes are firmly wedged, then tie them all together to prevent movement. If the row is long, the horizontal cane may not be long enough. Simply insert another cane and overlap the two for about 30cm (1ft).

5 Individual canes are very useful for plants such as tomatoes, but make sure 30–60cm (1–2ft) of the cane is pushed into the ground, otherwise it will not support the weight of a fruiting plant.

ROUTINE CARE

Regular weeding, feeding and watering will bring out the best in your vegetables. The increased yields always make the effort worthwhile.

WEEDING

1 Regular hoeing is the best way to keep down weeds between the rows. A Dutch hoe, used with a pushing motion, is very efficient. A wide head covers the ground more quickly, but is more difficult to manoeuvre among close plants.

2 Hand-weeding is inevitable if the weeds are growing so close to the crop plants that it is hazardous to use a hoe. Pull up the weed with one hand while holding the vegetable firmly to reduce root disturbance.

3 Some pernicious weeds, such as thistles and bindweed, will break off if you try to pull them up from between the vegetables, and the roots that are left will spread even further. If you are careful, you can eliminate difficult weeds by painting them with a translocated weedkiller such as glyphosate. If painted on to the leaves, it will kill the roots. But be very careful not to let it touch the crop plants.

FEEDING

1 A balanced fertilizer should be applied before sowing or planting. Sometimes, however, vegetables benefit from a boost of a specific fertilizer as the season progresses. Sprinkle it along the rows at the recommended rate, keeping it close to the roots but off the leaves. Hoe and/or water it in if the weather is dry.

2 Use liquid fertilizers to boost growth during the summer. Most plants will usually respond rapidly to a liquid feed at this time. Dilute according to the manufacturer's instructions, or apply through a hose-end dilutor.

WATERING

■ **Sprinkler** The best way to water a vegetable garden is with a sprinkler that distributes the water over a wide area. Most lawn sprinklers lack the height to clear tall nearby foliage with the spray. Buy one that has the head on top of a stalk or spike, so that the water is thrown well clear.

■ **Seep hose** Seep hoses (right) are effective for vegetables planted in rows. Once one row has been watered thoroughly, move the hose to the next one.

Seep hose

SPECIAL TECHNIQUES 1

Some vegetables – such as chicory and endive – are more succulent and less bitter if you blanch them. Rhubarb is forced in the dark to provide tender young stems earlier than normal.

GROWING AND FORCING CHICORY

1 To produce chicons (blanched heads) for winter use, sow a variety such as 'Witloof' in late spring or early summer. Lift the roots from mid autumn onwards, and leave them exposed for a couple of days to retard growth.

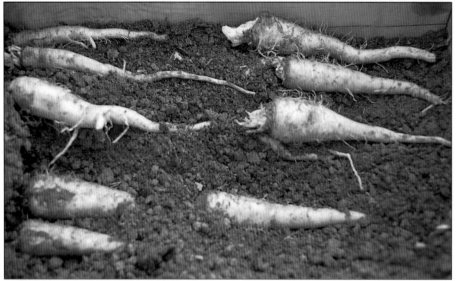

2 When the roots have dried, trim off the leaves about 2.5–5cm (1–2in) above the top of the root. If you have more roots than you want to force immediately, store the spare ones in a box of sand, peat or dry soil until ready to use.

3 **RIGHT** Trim the bottom off the root with a sharp knife so that it will fit into a 15–23cm (6–9in) pot. Place the roots in the pot and pack soil around them so that the shoulder of each root is just beneath the soil. Place a pot of the same size or a size larger over the top of the pot, and cover the holes (you can put a piece of kitchen foil inside the pot). Keep in a temperature of about 10°C (50°F) for about three weeks. Keep the compost moist but not wet, and harvest the chicons (blanched heads) when they are about 15cm (6in) tall.

1 To force rhubarb in the garden, place an old barrel, tea chest or other wooden box over a root in early or mid winter, or make a framework of wire netting and canes as shown.

2 If using a barrel or tea chest, you will get an earlier crop if you pile decomposing manure around the outside and over the top of the box to generate warmth. If using the wire netting method, pile straw into the cage to provide warmth and protection.

3 Another method is to use a plastic dustbin, either inverted or with the bottom cut out. Whichever method you use, check progress after a couple of months, and pull the stems when they are about 25–30cm (10–12in) long.

4 You can force the roots indoors, but first lift a crown (group of roots) at least two years old and leave it exposed to the cold for a few weeks. Place the crown in a black polythene sack and pack slightly moist peat or soil around the root or pot it up. If the soil is too wet, fungus diseases will be a problem. Secure the top of the bag with a large plastic-covered wire twist-tie, so that you can easily check on progress.

5 Place the sack in a warm place indoors until the forced stems are ready to harvest. Check periodically to make sure that the root or stems are not affected by fungus; if so, discard them.

BLANCHING ENDIVE

Grow endive as you would lettuce, but blanch the leaves so that they are not too bitter. About two weeks before they are ready to harvest, cover each plant with an old plate or a special plastic blanching dish sold especially for the purpose.

Remove the cover only when you are ready to eat the endive. The covered area will be pale but more succulent and less bitter.

FAR RIGHT Rhubarb is so easy and trouble-free to grow that we tend to take it for granted. But it makes a decorative foliage plant good enough to grow in a border, and the forced stems are a treat to enjoy early in the season.

SPECIAL TECHNIQUES 2

Don't give up trying to grow tomatoes if you don't have a greenhouse. In many areas you will achieve a good crop outdoors if you choose a suitable variety. In cold areas, try raising tomatoes in growing bags or pots in a porch. If you have been put off by the work involved in earthing up and lifting potatoes, grow them under black polythene.

CHITTING

If you chit the tubers you will have a crop several weeks earlier than you would otherwise.

Place the potatoes in trays and keep in a light, frost-free place.

When the shoots are about 2cm (¾in) long the tubers are ready to plant. Avoid long, thin shoots.

EARTHING UP

Potatoes not grown under black polythene have to be earthed up to prevent the tubers being exposed to the light. This will cause them to turn green and become inedible.

Earth up in stages as the plants grow. Use a draw hoe to mound soil up each side of the plants, taking it from the space between the rows.

POTATOES UNDER POLYTHENE

1 Roll out the black polythene over the prepared ground. Bury the edges to prevent the polythene blowing away. Make a shallow slit in the soil with a spade, push the sides in, then pull the soil back over the edge to secure.

2 Make slits through the polythene with a sharp knife, at an appropriate spacing for the potato variety. Plant the tubers through the slits. Use a trowel to plant the potatoes about 10cm (4in) deep through each slit.

3 Once the tops have died down, harvest the potatoes by lifting the black polythene. Most of the potatoes will be lying on the surface ready to harvest.

1 Plant tall varieties that need staking 38–45cm (15–18in) apart. The plants must have been well hardened off (acclimatized to outdoor conditions).

2 The plants will get off to a better start if you can protect them with large barn cloches initially, or cover with horticultural fleece.

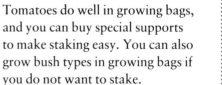

GROWING BAGS AND POTS

Tomatoes do well in growing bags, and you can buy special supports to make staking easy. You can also grow bush types in growing bags if you do not want to stake.

If you are not looking for a heavy crop, try growing suitable varieties in pots.

3 When the plants are too tall for the cloches, remove them and stake the plants. If you are not using cloches, stake immediately after planting. Push the stakes or canes well into the ground, one for each tomato plant.

4 Keep the main stem tied to the support as it grows. Remove all the sideshoots while they are still young. Pinch out the growing tip when it reaches the top of the cane. Fruits that develop on the top trusses often do not ripen outdoors anyway, so let the plant concentrate its energy into the lower trusses of fruit.

5 Dwarf and bush tomatoes sprawl over the ground and do not require staking. Plant them 30–75cm (1–2½ft) apart, depending on the variety. If possible cover these plants with a floating cloche, and remove it when you need to start harvesting the fruit, or when the plants grow too tall.

SPECIAL TECHNIQUES 3

Traditional trench varieties of celery require careful blanching, but if you find this too much of a chore you can grow the self-blanching type in blocks and let the plants blanch each other. Carrots can be an easy crop to grow, but if carrot fly usually devastates your crop beat it with a simple barrier.

BEATING CARROT FLY

If carrot fly is normally troublesome, instead of using soil insecticides – which have limited success – erect a barrier of polythene or very fine mesh netting around the seedlings while they are still small.

Make the barrier 60–90cm (2–3ft) high, as this is the height beyond which the pest does not normally fly. If the flies cannot lay their eggs around the seedlings, you will not have maggoty roots at harvest time.

SELF-BLANCHING CELERY

1 Plant self-blanching celery varieties in blocks rather than rows. The inner plants are then protected by the outer ones. Plant the celery 23cm (9in) apart to increase the blanching effect.

2 Harvest by lifting with a fork. You will have to discard more leaves from the heads on the outside of the block than in the inner part.

BLANCHING TRENCH CELERY

1 Trench varieties are usually planted in a trench to make blanching and watering easier. Excavate a trench as shown, and fork in as much organic matter, such as garden compost or manure, as possible.

2 Plant in two rows 30cm (1ft) apart, with about 25cm (10in) between the plants.

3 Keep the plants well watered. To facilitate this the trench can easily be flooded with water periodically in dry weather during the early stages of growth.

4 Some people earth up their celery with soil, but many gardeners prefer to blanch the stems with paper or drainpipes. Wrap corrugated cardboard or lightproof paper loosely around the stems. As the plants grow taller, you will have to add another layer higher up, overlapping the two slightly.

Special Techniques 4

POLLINATING MARROWS AND COURGETTES

1 Marrows and courgettes – which are immature marrows – are usually pollinated by insects, but hand-pollination may be necessary if the weather is cold or fruits are not forming for some other reason. You can identify the female flower (left) by the small swelling, which is the embryonic fruit, behind the flower.

2 To pollinate a marrow or courgette, take a male flower that is fully open, remove its petals to make insertion easier, then press it against the stigma of the female flower.

3 Alternatively, use a small paintbrush to gather pollen from the male flower, then brush it on to the stigma of the female.

4 Harvest courgettes while they are still young – about 10cm (4in) long. The more frequently you pick them, the more fruits the plant will produce.

GROWING ONIONS FROM SETS

1 Take out shallow drills about 30cm (12in) apart using a hoe and garden line. Space the onion sets about 15cm (6in) apart in the drills. If necessary press them firmly into the soil so just the tips will protrude above the soil when the drills are filled in.

2 Pull the soil back into the drills with a rake, so the onion sets are covered and just the tips protrude. If birds cause a problem by pulling the sets out of the ground or loosen them by tugging on the wispy old stems that poke through the soil, protect the onions until they form roots. Use wire-netting or criss-cross black cotton strung between short pegs over the area planted.

ENSURING SWEET CORN POLLINATION

1 Sweet corn is wind-pollinated, and has separate male and female flowers. The male flowers are at the top of the plant, and the female (above) below. The female flowers are the ones that will develop into the cobs.

2 Because sweet corn is pollinated by the wind, you will increase your chances of fertile cobs if you plant in blocks rather than long rows.

3 Press a fingernail into a kernel to test whether a cob is ready for harvesting. If a milky liquid oozes out, the cob is ready. If the liquid looks watery it is under-ripe; if the kernel is mealy it's over-ripe.

Vegetables such as onions and courgettes are easy to grow, especially if you plant onion sets.

GREENHOUSE VEGETABLES 1 : TOMATOES

Tomatoes are a popular greenhouse crop, and you should be able to harvest them over a long season. If you have a heated greenhouse start them early, but if your greenhouse is unheated do not plant until you are sure it will be frost-free.

TOMATOES IN BORDERS

1 RIGHT It is worth trying tomatoes in the greenhouse border for a couple of years. After that, either replace the soil every year or two, or use one of the other methods described. This will avoid problems from soil-borne pests and diseases. Plant about 45cm (18in) apart from late winter onwards in a heated greenhouse, or in late spring or early summer in an unheated greenhouse.

Tomatoes need regular feeding. Use a specially formulated liquid tomato feed for best results – some are intended for use during early growth, while others have a high potassium content for ripening fruits.

RING CULTURE

1 Ring culture is worth considering once the border soil ceases to be productive, or if soil-borne pests and diseases have become troublesome. Take out a trench in the border and line it with polythene to reduce the risk of contamination from the underlying soil.

2 Place fine gravel or coarse grit in the lined trench, and place special ring culture bottomless pots on top.

3 Fill the bottomless pots with a good loam-based compost and plant the tomatoes in this. Water only into the rings, but once the plants are established and some roots have penetrated the aggregate below, feed through the pot but water through the aggregate.

2 Although you can use canes for support, string is a more economical method of supporting the plants.

3 As the tomatoes grow, gently loop the string around the growing tip so that it forms a spiral around the plant. Suspend the string from the roof.

4 Snap off the sideshoots, and any shoots growing from the base, while they are still small. Pull sideways to snap them off cleanly.

5 If fruits are failing to form through poor pollination (sometimes a problem early in the season), either shake the plants each day, or mist the flowers with water. Both techniques help to spread the pollen.

6 Remove any yellowing lower leaves as the plants grow tall. These will not contribute to feeding the plant, and removing them will allow more light to reach the fruits.

7 Harvest the fruit when it is just ripe, and pick it with the green calyx attached.

8 RIGHT When six or seven sprays of fruit have set, remove the growing tip two leaves above the top spray of flowers. Late fruits are unlikely to ripen well unless you heat your greenhouse in the autumn. It is better to encourage the plant to put its energy into the fruits that will mature.

GROWING BAGS

1 Growing bags also provide an alternative to a contaminated border, but careful watering and feeding are essential. Plant three tomatoes in a standard-sized bag. Do not try to pack too many into a limited amount of compost.

2 Proprietary cane supports can be used, but in the greenhouse there are cheaper options. Push the canes through the bottom of the bag into the border below (there is only a slight risk of diseases entering through the hole), or use strings suspended from the roof (*see* Tomatoes in Borders).

BUSH VARIETIES

The advice given above is for cordon or indeterminate varieties. Bush varieties are not normally grown as a greenhouse crop, but if you choose one you will not need to provide the normal support, and you should not pinch out the sideshoots.

GREENHOUSE VEGETABLES 2: AUBERGINES, CUCUMBERS, MELONS AND SWEET PEPPERS

All these vegetables are easy to grow in a greenhouse, and make a change from tomatoes. It is sometimes recommended that you avoid growing these different crops together, but in an amateur greenhouse where a little compromise is acceptable you can grow any combination of them.

BELOW Aubergines are decorative plants, and will make a change from tomatoes in your greenhouse.

AUBERGINES

1 Aubergines can be grown in growing bags or in pots. They do well in 20cm (8in) pots containing a loam-based compost. Pinch out the growing tip when the plant is about 30cm (12in) tall, to encourage the sideshoots to develop.

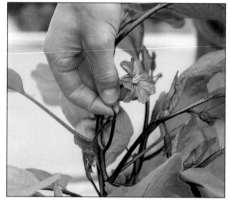

2 Allow only one aubergine fruit to develop on each shoot. Remove the other flowers and pinch out the growing tips of the shoots at about three leaves beyond the developing fruit.

3 Make sure that the plant never goes short of nutrients or water. Aubergines also benefit from high humidity, so regular misting is beneficial.

4 The fruits can be heavy, so stake varieties that grow taller than 60cm (2ft). Aubergines usually have purple fruits, but some are white. Harvest with at least 2.5cm (1in) of the stalk attached.

CUCUMBERS

1 Bush varieties can simply be allowed to sprawl, but most greenhouse varieties are trained to canes and wires. Plant in the greenhouse border or in growing bags – two in a standard-sized bag. Insert one upright cane for each plant, and stretch horizontal wires 15cm (6in) apart about 30cm (12in) away from the glass.

2 Tie the main stem to the cane at regular intervals, and pinch out the growing tip when it reaches the roof.

3 Many modern varieties produce only female flowers, but if you grow one that produces males too be sure to pinch these out. Female flowers have a small embryo fruit behind the petals, while male flowers do not have this swelling.

4 Tie the sideshoots to the horizontal wires. Once tiny cucumbers appear on them, pinch out the shoots just beyond two leaves after the fruit. Feed and water regularly, and keep the atmosphere humid.

SWEET PEPPERS

Grow sweet peppers as described for aubergines, in pots or growing bags. Provide a stake, and pinch out the growing tip when the plants reach 60cm (2ft).

MELONS

1 Plant in a cool or heated greenhouse in late May, in growing bags or the greenhouse border. Provide a vertical cane for each plant and stretch horizontal wires about 30cm (12in) apart, 38cm (15in) in from the glass.

2 As the plant grows, tie the sideshoots to the horizontal wires. Pinch out the tip of the plant when it reaches 1.8m (6ft).

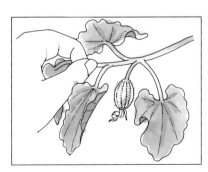

Pinch back all sideshoots on each melon plant to two leaves beyond each flower. If necessary, pollinate the flowers by hand. Transfer the pollen from male to female flowers with a small paintbrush. If many fruits form, thin to four on each plant. As they enlarge, support them in net slings.

PATIO VEGETABLES

You can grow a surprisingly wide selection of vegetables even if you have no more than a backyard or balcony. Some are attractive enough in containers to make pleasant patio plants.

GROWING BAGS

1 Growing bags can be used for many vegetables, even potatoes. It isn't practical to grow maincrop potatoes in them because you will not crop enough to keep the family supplied, but grow a few earlies to enjoy at the beginning of the potato season. Do not open the bag in the normal way, but just cut slits large enough to plant the tubers – it is the equivalent of planting beneath black polythene.

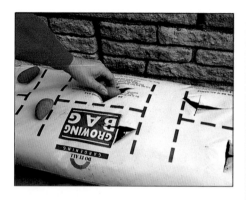

2 Keep the plants well watered, and feed occasionally with a liquid fertilizer.

3 A single growing bag will produce a respectable crop of potatoes, and they are fun to grow.

4 Spinach and self-blanching celery are among the leaf and stem crops that are also practical for a growing bag. Sow directly into the bag, or plant as seedlings, depending on the vegetable concerned.

5 Peas and dwarf French beans are also suitable crops. Choose dwarf varieties and sow directly into the growing bag.

6 **RIGHT** Many salad crops can be grown in this way. Lettuces are a popular crop, but try salad onions and even beetroot too. Tomatoes are, of course, a popular crop for growing bags.

FRUIT & VEGETABLES

WINDOWBOXES

1 If you want to grow tomatoes but only have space for them in a windowbox, grow a miniature or tumbling variety. These can also be grown in hanging baskets, but are easier to look after in a windowbox.

2 Lettuces grow well in windowboxes, but choose a cut-and-come-again variety, such as 'Salad Bowl' or 'Red Salad Bowl' if you don't want your box to look bare when you decide to start harvesting. Just pick enough leaves for one meal at a time and take care not to strip any plant completely.

TUBS AND POTS

1 Many tomato varieties are suitable for growing in tubs or large pots. Plant in late spring or early summer. Be prepared to protect from late frosts. Feed regularly. Use a liquid tomato fertilizer if you can remember to feed regularly, otherwise add a slow-release or controlled-release fertilizer to the compost when planting.

2 Even compact varieties suitable for pots can supply a useful crop of tomatoes.

3 Courgettes and bush cucumbers do well in tubs or large pots, and a yellow variety of courgette will look very attractive too.

HARVESTING AND STORING

Don't let your vegetables go to waste because you have not harvested and stored them properly. Many can be stored in good condition for weeks or even months and will provide a constant supply for the winter.

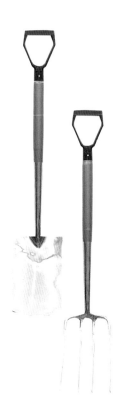

MAKING AN ONION ROPE

1 You can store onions in nets, which is quick and easy, but an onion rope looks more attractive. Start with a rope of the appropriate length, and make sure the onions have been harvested with their dried stems intact.

2 Starting at the bottom, tie the onions to the rope by wrapping garden twine around the neck of each onion and the rope, tying each one in place securely.

3 Hang the completed ropes in a cool place where air can circulate freely around them.

PROTECTING CAULIFLOWER CURDS

If left unprotected, cauliflower curds like this soon discolour in bright sunlight in summer, and are easily damaged by frost in winter. Fold over the leaves to keep them looking good for longer.

When the curd is almost mature, fold over some of the largest leaves to protect it. Bend the leaf enough to break it without snapping it off completely. The protected head will then last in good condition for longer.

For winter protection, tie the outer leaves with string to hold them over the curd as protection. This is more important with old varieties than modern ones, which have been bred to have leaves that curl over the centre anyway.

PICKING BRUSSELS SPROUTS

Varieties bred for freezing tend to have sprouts that mature along the stem at about the same time, but other varieties usually mature in succession. Pick the lowest sprouts first, snapping them off, and leave the smaller sprouts at the top to grow larger. At the same time snap off any yellowing or diseased leaves. This will reduce the likelihood of fungal diseases affecting the remaining sprouts.

STORING CARROTS AND BEETROOT

1 If you have grown a lot of carrots or beetroot and have been unable to keep up with them, lift them before they deteriorate in the ground or get eaten by pests. They will be safer if lifted and stored.

2 Twist off the leaves, otherwise they may make the roots rot.

BELOW Bought vegetables never taste quite so good as those freshly lifted, especially early in the season. But it is worth storing them for winter use.

3 Make an improvised store, either in a large box inside a cool shed or outside like the one shown here. Lay the roots on damp sand or peat, making sure that they do not actually touch each other. Build up the store layer by layer, with moist sand or peat between each one. Cover with about 15cm (6in) of soil or sand.

STORING POTATOES

1 Lift potatoes for storing after the foliage has died down. Use a fork and shake them free of soil.

2 Leave the potatoes on the surface of the ground for a couple of hours to allow the soil and skins to dry off.

3 Sort the tubers before storing. Discard the smallest or use them up very quickly, keep the middle-sized ones for eating during the next few weeks, and store only the largest. Potatoes must be kept frost-free, preferably in lightproof sacks in a cool but frost-free shed or garage. Paper sacks are better than polythene ones, but the latter can be used if you make some ventilation holes with a sharp knife. The potatoes must be dry before storing.

STORING WINTER CABBAGES

Winter white cabbages and red cabbages will usually stand in the garden for weeks and remain usable, but it is best to harvest most of them while they are still in good condition, then store them in a cool but frost-free place. Strip off the coarse outer leaves before you store them.

Store them in a cool place such as a cellar, shed or garage, preferably just above freezing and

well-ventilated. Place them on a slatted bench (straw will help to protect them, but it's not essential), or hang them in nets.

Vegetable Facts At Your Fingertips

Use this table as a quick reference guide for advice on how to grow all the common vegetables. The dates are for the most popular varieties and methods of cultivation: these may vary for specific varieties or techniques. Always check the seed packet or planting instructions for dates and spacings.

VEGETABLE	SOW	PLANT	HARVEST	REMARKS
ARTICHOKE, GLOBE	Mid/late spring	Spring	Early summer to mid autumn	Usually propagated by root division but can be raised from seed (no harvest first year)
ARTICHOKE, JERUSALEM	Plant tubers	Early/mid spring	Mid summer to following spring	Grows to 3m (10ft). Reduce height to 1.5m (5ft) in late summer to reduce risk of wind damage. A smooth rather than knobbly variety is easier to prepare
ASPARAGUS	Early/mid spring	Spring	Late spring	Seed-raised plants are variable. Best to plant year-old crowns of named varieties
AUBERGINE	Late winter/early spring	Early summer	Late summer/early autumn	Best grown in greenhouse or under cloches except in very mild regions
BEAN, BROAD	Spring or early autumn	Sow *in situ*	Summer	Choose a suitable variety if sowing in autumn, and if possible protect with a cloche. Pinch out growing tips once flowering starts
BEAN, FRENCH	Late spring/early summer	Sow *in situ*	Summer	Protect from frost
BEAN, RUNNER	Late spring/early summer	Early summer	Summer	Best sown *in situ*, but can be started off in pots. Needs support
BEETROOT	Late spring to mid summer	Sow *in situ*	Summer and autumn	Make several sowings several weeks apart
BROCCOLI, SPROUTING	Mid/late spring	Early/mid summer	Late winter to mid spring	
BRUSSELS SPROUT	Late winter to mid spring	Spring	Late summer to early winter	
CABBAGE, CHINESE	Late spring/mid summer	Summer	Mid summer to late autumn	Keep well watered
CABBAGE, SPRING	Late summer	Autumn	Spring	
CABBAGE, SUMMER/ AUTUMN	Early to late spring	Spring/summer	Summer/autumn	

VEGETABLE	SOW	PLANT	HARVEST	REMARKS
CABBAGE, WINTER	Spring	Late spring/summer	Winter	
CALABRESE	Late winter to late spring	Sow *in situ*	Early summer to mid autumn	
CAPSICUM	Late winter to early spring	Early summer	Mid summer to mid autumn	Best grown in a greenhouse or under a cloche, unless in a warm region
CARROT	Early spring to early summer	Sow *in situ*	Mid summer to mid autumn	
CAULIFLOWER, EARLY SUMMER	Autumn or late winter (under glass)	Spring	Early summer	
CAULIFLOWER, SUMMER/AUTUMN	Mid to late spring	Early summer	Summer and autumn	
CAULIFLOWER, WINTER	Late spring	Summer	Winter (mild areas) or spring	
CELERIAC	Early/mid spring	Late spring	Early/mid autumn	
CELERY	Early/mid spring	Late spring	Late summer to late autumn	
CHICORY, FOR CHICONS	Late spring/early summer	Sow *in situ*	Winter	
CHICORY, HEARTING TYPE	Summer	Sow *in situ*	Autumn	
CORN SALAD (LAMB'S LETTUCE)	Spring to autumn	Sow *in situ*	Summer, autumn, winter	
CUCUMBER, INDOOR	Late winter to late spring	Spring or early summer	Summer to mid autumn	
CUCUMBER, OUTDOOR	Spring	Late spring or early summer	Summer	

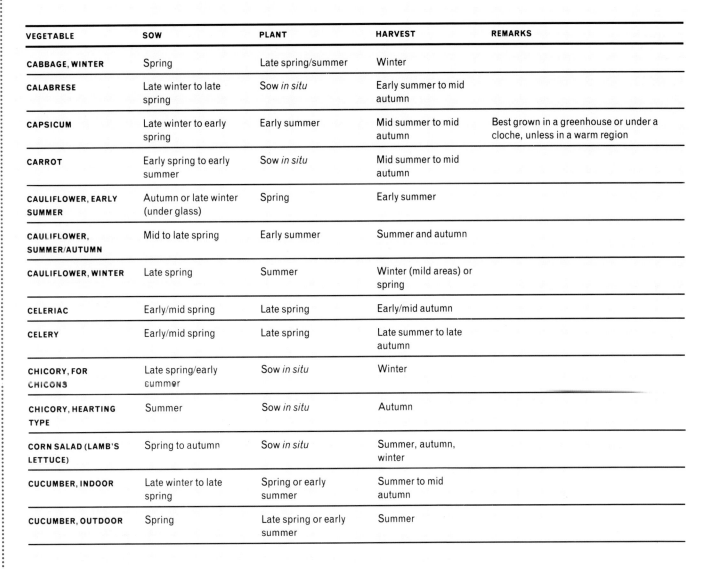

VEGETABLE	SOW	PLANT	HARVEST	REMARKS
ENDIVE	Mid spring to mid summer	Sow *in situ*	Mid summer to late autumn	
KALE	Mid or late spring	Late spring or early summer	Autumn and winter	
KOHL RABI	Early spring to early summer	Sow *in situ*	Early summer to mid autumn	
LEEK	Mid winter to mid spring	Late spring or early summer	Mid autumn to early spring	
LETTUCE	Early spring to mid summer	Late spring to mid summer	Early summer to mid autumn	By choosing suitable varieties and sowing at the times recommended for them, it is possible to harvest lettuce all year round by using cloches, frames or a greenhouse
MARROW, PUMPKIN, SQUASH, COURGETTE	Mid or late spring	Late spring or early summer	Mid summer to mid autumn	
MELON	Late winter/early spring	Late spring/early summer	Mid summer to mid autumn	
ONION	Late winter to mid spring	Early/mid spring	Mid summer to mid autumn	Can be raised from seed or 'sets' (small bulbs)
ONION, JAPANESE	Mid summer to early autumn	Sow *in situ*	Early spring to mid summer	Not recommended for areas where winters are very cold or very wet
ONION, SPRING OR BUNCHING	Early spring to early autumn	Sow *in situ*	Late spring to late autumn – those sown in late summer and early autumn are ready in spring	
PARSNIP	Late winter to mid spring	Sow *in situ*	Mid autumn to late winter	
PEA	Early spring to early summer	Sow *in situ*	Summer	Some varieties can be sown in autumn in mild areas to harvest in late spring and early summer
POTATO	Plant tubers	Mid or late spring	Early summer to late autumn	

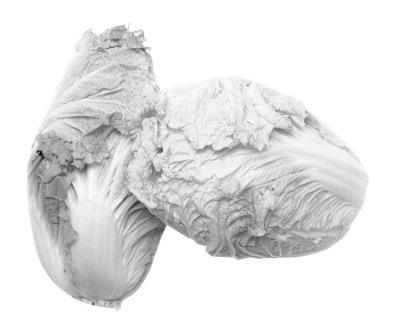

VEGETABLE	SOW	PLANT	HARVEST	REMARKS
RADISH	Early spring to early autumn	Sow *in situ*	Mid spring to late autumn	
RADISH, WINTER	Mid summer to mid autumn	Sow *in situ*	Mid autumn to early winter	
SALSIFY	Early to late spring	Sow *in situ*	Mid autumn to late winter	
SCORZONERA	Mid/late spring	Sow *in situ*	Mid autumn to early spring	
SHALLOT	Plant sets (bulbs)	Late winter to mid spring	Mid summer to early autumn	
SPINACH	Late winter to mid summer	Sow *in situ*	Late spring to mid autumn	Sow successionally
SPINACH, NEW ZEALAND	Spring	Sow *in situ*	Mid summer to mid autumn	
SWEDE	Late spring/early summer	Sow *in situ*	Mid autumn to early spring	
SWEET CORN	Mid/late spring	Late spring/early summer	Late summer/early autumn	
SWISS CHARD	Early spring to mid summer	Sow *in situ*	Mid summer to mid autumn	
TOMATO, INDOOR	Mid winter to early spring	Early to late spring	Early summer to mid autumn	
TOMATO, OUTDOOR	Early or mid spring	Late spring/early summer	Mid summer to mid autumn	
TURNIP	Early spring to early summer	Sow *in situ*	Early summer to mid autumn	

GROWING HERBS

Few gardeners have space for a proper formal herb garden, but you can create attractive mini herb gardens in a small space, and the more ornamental herbs are easily integrated into flower beds and borders.

MAKING A HERB WHEEL

1 A herb wheel is an attractive feature that will enable you to grow a small collection of herbs without making a more elaborate herb garden. If you are lucky enough to have an old cartwheel, paint this, lay it on the ground and plant different herbs between the spokes. To make a brick equivalent, mark a circle of the appropriate diameter – about 1.5m (5ft) across, or larger if you have space for a centrepiece (something like an upright rosemary or simply a striking ornament). Excavate the circle to a depth of about 15cm (6in).

2 Lay a circle of bricks on end or at an angle to create an attractive dog-tooth effect. It may be necessary to adjust the diameter of the circle slightly for a close fit. If you want to make a good job of your herb wheel, lift the bricks after laying them loosely, make a shallow concrete foundation, and when that has set mortar the bricks into place. Otherwise compact the earth around each brick, checking levels with a spirit-level.

3 Lay lines of bricks as the 'spokes'. Leave plenty of planting space between each spoke. Do not worry if the bricks do not meet exactly in the centre. Mask any gap with a plant or an ornament – or an attractive pot containing herbs.

4 Top up the soil between the spokes with a loam-based potting compost, or good garden soil.

5 Plant up your herb wheel with a collection of herbs that you will use and that are ornamental. If you choose perennials, you will not have to replant each spring.

6 For an attractive finishing touch, cover the surface around the plants with stone chippings or cocoa shells.

PLANNING FOR WINTER

1 Pot up a few herbs that are small enough and that will continue to grow for a few more months indoors. Chives can be treated this way.

2 Pot up in a 15–20cm (6–8in) pot, water well, and keep by a light window.

3 Lift some mint before it dies back in autumn. Pot up in a 20–25cm (8–10in) pot, and keep on a light window-sill.

HERBS IN CONTAINERS

If space is limited, or you want to grow your herbs on the patio or by the back door, containers offer plenty of scope.

GROWING BAGS

1 Mints do well in growing bags, and this is an ideal way to ensure they do not invade the rest of the garden. You can plant a small collection of perhaps four different mints in a growing bag. Even a single growing bag will yield enough mint or sorrel (also a good candidate for a growing bag) for a typical family. Just harvest enough leaves for your immediate needs.

2 Growing bags are suitable for many low-growing annual herbs, such as parsley and summer savory.

PLANTING A BARREL OR TUB

1 Use a large container such as a half-barrel or large tub for such shrubby herbs as bay. Make sure there are drainage holes in the bottom of the container, and use a good loam-based compost.

2 If the plant looks small for the size of container, plant a decorative edging of a compact herb such as golden marjoram or golden thyme all around it.

PLANTING A HERB POT

1 Herb pots look attractive, but always bear in mind the ultimate size and spread of each herb when planting. Put small plants such as thymes or parsley in the planting pockets. Fill the pot with compost to that level, introduce the roots, then add more compost. Do not plant a potentially large shrub in the top of the pot as it will be difficult to remove a year or two later. Choose something attractive yet fairly shallow-rooting, such as chives.

2 A herb pot like this is a very decorative feature, so harvest just a few leaves or flowers from each plant to avoid spoiling the overall effect.

WINDOWBOXES

Herbs can make attractive windowbox plants, but try to choose compact types such as marjorams, parsley and mints (variegated apple mint looks good). Young shrubby plants such as sages can be used, but be prepared to replant every year or two.

HARVESTING AND STORING HERBS

Herbs are best harvested fresh, but many can be dried or preserved in other ways to enjoy when fresh herbs are not available.

COLLECTING FRESH HERBS

1 Herbs such as basil, tarragon and marjoram will become bushier and a better shape if you harvest the growing tips first. Later, harvest the larger side leaves.

2 Pick the outer leaves from parsley, sorrel, lovage and salad burnet first. More leaves will continue to grow from the centre of the plant.

3 Harvest leaves and sprigs from shrubby herbs, such as rosemary, thyme and sage, from positions that will not spoil the shape of the plant. Try not to harvest too heavily from one part of the plant.

4 Harvest chives and Welsh onions by cutting them down to about 4cm (1½in) with scissors. The leaves will regrow, but remove only as many as you need rather than cut down the whole plant.

Although most herbs are best used fresh, as soon as possible after picking, most can also be dried or frozen. All the herbs shown here (left to right: dill, thyme, mint, rosemary, parsley, and sage) can be dried.

AIR DRYING

1 Hang those herbs that can be cut as sprigs to dry in an airy place. Tie them in small bunches. They will probably be dry enough to store after a week, but if you are likely to use them fairly soon, just leave them hanging in bunches.

2 Dry individual leaves on a wire rack, so that air can circulate around them. For small leaves, cover the rack with muslin or cheesecloth. Do not wash the leaves, but wipe off any grit or soil. Leave them in a warm, dark place for about a week (up to two weeks in cool temperatures).

3 Store in glass bottles (dark glass is best). Plastic and metal containers can affect the chemistry of some herbs. Remember to label them carefully.

FREEZING

1 Many herbs are suitable for freezing in ice cubes. Chopped parsley, chopped chives, mint and lemon balm leaves all freeze well. Borage flowers make decorative ice cubes for summer drinks. Use equal measures of chopped herbs and water. For whole leaves or flowers, just push them into the trays of water.

2 Soft-leaved herbs such as basil, parsley and sweet Cicely can be frozen dry in bags. Pack whole sprigs into labelled freezer bags and place in the freezer. The herbs will crumble easily once frozen. If you plan to store them for a long time, blanch them, then pat dry before freezing.

Growing Fruit

Fruit growing can be a rewarding hobby, and you do not need an orchard or a very large garden to be able to enjoy a surprisingly wide selection of home-grown fruits. You can even grow a small apple tree in a patio pot, strawberries can be grown successfully in containers on a balcony, and cordon-trained apples and pears look good against the garden fence.

CHOOSING A SITE
Almost all fruits prefer a sunny position. It is also important to avoid frost pockets. Cold air tends

to collect in pockets on low-lying ground, especially in valleys if there is no outlet for it. You will suffer poor crops if frost damages the blossom on trees like apples and pears. The latter are particularly vulnerable as they flower earlier than apples. If growing fruit trees in a mixed kitchen garden, place them where they will not cast shade over the vegetables.

FRUITFUL IDEAS
If you don't have space for a small orchard in your garden, grow trained fruit trees, such as fans,

cordons or espaliers, against a wall or fence. They look decorative and take up little room.

Ballerina apple trees grow as a narrow column, even without pruning, and make an ornamental feature both in flower and fruit. Minimal pruning is required, so they are a good choice if you dislike the thought of regular pruning.

Some fruits can be grown successfully in tubs or pots on the patio, or in any other place where they will make an attractive feature. If you choose an apple tree for a tub, make sure that it has been grafted to a very dwarfing rootstock. Peaches also make attractive tub plants on the patio in warmer areas, but avoid very vigorous trees such as pears.

You can even grow an apple as a decorative edging to a bed, perhaps in the kitchen garden. Step-over

With modern varieties and training techniques, you don't need a large garden to grow apples. The step-over method (left) makes an ornamental edging. 'Ballerina' apples (bottom of opposite page) grow into narrow columns.

BELOW It's easy to grow a wide range of fruit in the garden, including blackcurrants, redcurrants, strawberries, raspberries and gooseberries.

apples are single-armed espaliers.

Even rampant fruits like blackberries, as well as hybrid berries, can be trained to look neat. They won't become overgrown, or be difficult to pick at harvest time, if they are trained to wires stretched between stout posts.

Some fruits look good trained over an arch. Apples pruned like cordons can be trained over a strong arch instead of against angled canes. Blackberries and hybrid berries can be trained over an arch, but the thorns can be a hazard for unsuspecting passers-by.

FRUIT & VEGETABLES

PLANTING A FRUIT TREE OR BUSH 1

Fruit trees and bushes will be in the ground for a long time, and you get only one chance to plant them properly. Prepare the ground well beforehand, and take care with the planting so that your fruit gets off to a good start.

PLANTING A CORDON OR ESPALIER

1 Fix the supporting wires first. Space the wires horizontally about 30–45cm (12–18in) apart, and 10–15cm (4–6in) away from the wall or fence. If planting a cordon, firmly secure a cane at an angle of 45° where the plant will be.

2 Prepare the ground thoroughly as for a free-standing tree, but plant the tree with the stem about 23cm (9in) away from the wall or fence. Place a cane across the planting hole to check that the level of the soil will reach the old soil mark on the tree after planting. If planting a cordon, make sure that the stem is in a position where it can be tied to the cane.

PLANTING A FREE-STANDING TREE

1 Make sure that the ground is free of weeds, and incorporate garden compost or well-rotted manure. Excavate a hole at least one-third larger than the width of the container (the bigger the better), and fork over the bottom so that the plant does not sit on compacted ground.

2 If using a container-grown tree, remove it from its container, and test the root ball for size and depth. Add more soil to the planting hole or remove as necessary. If using a stake, insert it to one side of the hole *before* you plant the tree.

3 If planting a container-grown tree, tease out some of the roots if they are tightly wound around the edge of the root ball, to encourage them to grow out. Return the soil, but enrich it with compost or well-rotted manure, and a slow-release fertilizer if necessary.

4 Tread the soil firmly with your feet to remove any large pockets of air.

5 Hoe the firmed soil to remove your footprints, and mulch the surface to conserve moisture and suppress weeds.

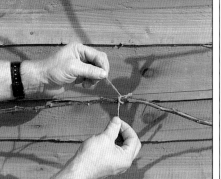

3 Mix a slow-release fertilizer into the soil to be returned to the planting hole. Rake the ground level, then firm with your feet to remove air pockets. Hoe out your footprints.

4 If planting a cordon, tie the stem to the oblique cane in several places to ensure that it grows at the correct angle. If planting an espalier, tie the main stem upright, securing any horizontal branches to the wires (make sure that the wires are at the appropriate heights if you buy a tree with the initial training already done).

1 Prepare the ground as described for trees, always remembering to make the hole wider than the roots or root ball. Use a cane to check that the bush is planted at its original depth.

BELOW Every garden has space for some fruit – a cordon pear like this can be grown against a wall or fence.

2 After firming the soil around the plant, hoe and rake to remove compressed footprints. If planting in spring, rake in a balanced fertilizer at the same time.

3 Most bushes which are grown on stems that sprout from a low base, such as blackcurrants, are best cut back hard after planting. This will stimulate new shoots from low down.

PLANTING A BARE-ROOTED TREE

If planting a bare-rooted tree, spread the roots out as widely as possible in the planting hole. If necessary, enlarge the hole to accommodate them.

PLANTING A FRUIT TREE 2

Trees need staking initially, but using an inappropriate stake or an unsuitable tree tie can do more harm than good. In very exposed gardens, or for trees that are particularly large when you plant them, a different staking method may be more appropriate, but the techniques here are adequate for the majority of trees likely to be planted in ordinary gardens.

STAKING A FRUIT TREE

1 A low stake like this is now considered better than a tall one, as the flexing of the stem in the wind can help to strengthen it. Insert the stake when planting, if possible placing it on the side of the prevailing wind so the tree is not blown against the stake. For stability make sure at least 60cm (2ft) of the stake is in the ground.

2 You can improvise a tree tie, but if possible use a proprietary tie that is easily adjusted and has a spacer to hold the stem away from the stake. Thread the tie through the spacer and around the tree before returning it through the other slot in the spacer.

ROOTSTOCKS

The vigour and size of your fruit tree will depend largely on the roots (rootstock) used when the variety was grafted. Trained trees like fans and cordons will almost certainly have been grafted on to an appropriate rootstock by the nursery, but for bush and standard trees you need to make sure that you choose one with an appropriate rootstock.

The illustration shows the relative heights for an apple tree of the same age on different rootstocks. M27 is very dwarfing, and suitable for trees in containers, M9 is a good choice for small garden trees, and M26 is suitable if you have space for a larger tree.

A dwarfing rootstock is useful for cherries and plums if you have a small garden. The cherry rootstock called 'Colt', for

example, will reduce the tree's size by about one-third (and it will crop sooner). Most plums sold in garden centres will have been grafted on to a dwarfing rootstock, but if you need a very dwarf tree look for 'Pixy' rootstock.

The rootstocks available may vary in different countries, and new ones are sometimes introduced, so if in doubt simply ask about the characteristics of the rootstock before you buy.

These are the likely heights of apples grown on different rootstocks. The more dwarfing the rootstock, the lighter the crop is likely to be, but the tree will probably start fruiting sooner and may make it possible to grow fruit in a garden that would otherwise be too small.

<u>3</u> Make sure the tree is held firmly against the spacer without allowing too much movement, which could damage the bark.

<u>4</u> Check the ties every year, and as soon as one begins to show signs of marking the bark where the trunk has expanded, loosen it to allow for further growth. You can untie most fruit trees after about three years of staking.

<u>5</u> Apply a mulch to suppress weeds and conserve moisture. Chipped bark is long-lasting and looks good, but you can use other materials instead. Make sure organic mulches like this are spread at least 5cm (2in) thick.

<u>6</u> If rabbits or other animals are a problem in your garden, use a tree guard to protect the trunk. Rabbits can kill a young tree by stripping off the bark.

ABOVE Most fruit trees benefit from initial staking, and especially those grown on very dwarfing rootstocks. Although staking is most useful for the first year or two when the trees are becoming established, do not forget to check the ties annually: they may have to be loosened to prevent the ties biting into the stem.

PRUNING TRAINED APPLES AND PEARS

Intensively trained apples and pears grown as cordons and espaliers must be pruned regularly – in summer and winter – to retain their shape and encourage cropping.

OPPOSITE Apples and pears trained against a wall or fence can look very attractive. This is an espalier-trained pear: the pretty blossom will be followed by a heavy crop of tasty fruit.

PRUNING A CORDON

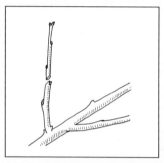

1 Shorten any long shoots that have grown since summer pruning. Prune only the sideshoots which are more than 10cm (4in) long, cutting them back to about 5cm (2in).

2 To avoid the shoots becoming congested and the fruits overcrowded, thin the spurs (stubs of old shoots) while the plant is dormant. This is not necessary on young plants – only on those where the spurs have become congested with age.

3 Remove the weakest and most congested spurs first, and leave those remaining well spaced (compare with the illustration for step 2).

4 When the main stem has reached the required height, and the cane has been lowered once to provide extra growing space, annual tipping back is needed. Prune the main stem back to within 12mm (½in) of the old wood, or to leave the new growth with one leaf.

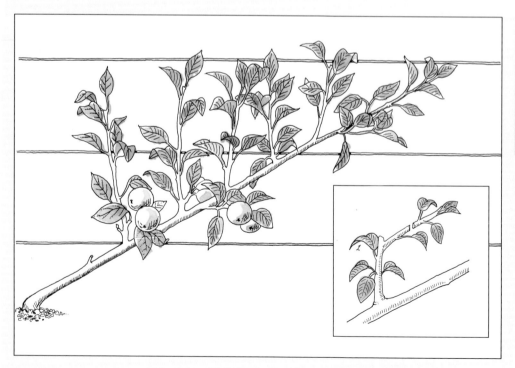

5 In late summer prune the sideshoots that grow from the main stem, but wait until they have become brown and woody at the base. Prune back to three leaves above the basal cluster of leaves.

6 **LEFT** At the same time, prune all shoots over 23cm (9in) long growing from spurs: cut back to one leaf above the basal cluster of leaves.

PRUNING AN ESPALIER

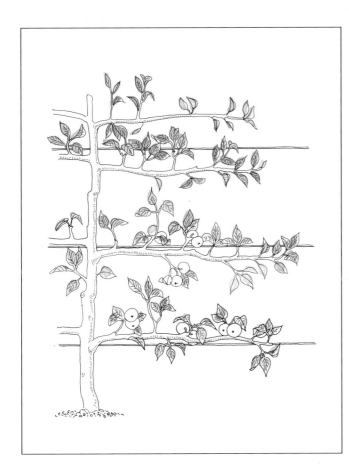

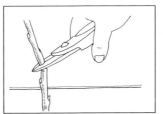

1 When the plant is dormant, thin out overcrowded spurs, removing the weakest and most congested. This will be necessary only on well established espaliers. If the tree is young, cut the main stem back to a bud just above the wire, to direct future growth into the horizontal branches.

2 In late summer, when this year's shoots are brown and woody at the base, start the summer pruning. Cut any shoots more than 23cm (9in) long, and growing directly from the tiered branches, to three leaves above the basal cluster of leaves.

3 Also cut any sideshoots of a similar length, that are growing from a cluster of spurs, back to one leaf above the basal cluster of leaves.

4 By early autumn more growth will probably have taken place. Cut any secondary growth back to one leaf from its base.

PRUNING A BUSH OR STANDARD APPLE OR PEAR TREE

There are many ways to prune apple and pear trees, but the methods shown here are easy if pruning has been carried out regularly. They are suitable for bush and standard trees (these have rounded heads, but the bush has only a very short trunk). If the flowers and fruit on your tree grow mainly in clusters along the shoots, follow the advice for spur pruning. If, however, the fruit grows mainly at the tips of the shoots, follow the advice for pruning a tip bearer.

Bush apples are not difficult to prune and usually give a high yield.

BARK RINGING

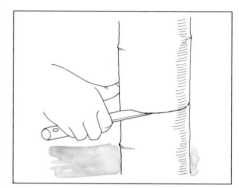

1 Bark ringing will help to reduce the vigour of a strong apple or pear, and may stimulate a poorly fruiting tree to produce a better crop. Make two parallel cuts 3–6mm (⅛–¼in) apart, deep enough to penetrate the bark and cambium layer (to the hard wood beneath). Do this in late spring, and never make the cut too wide otherwise you may kill the tree.

SPUR PRUNING

1 While the tree is dormant, prune each branch in turn. Cut the sideshoots that have grown during the summer months to between three and six buds.

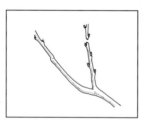

2 Shorten the tip of the main shoot by cutting back the summer's growth by between one-third and one-quarter.

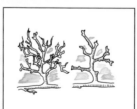

3 If the spurs have become very congested by years of growth and pruning, thin them out. Cut out the weakest and most congested ones first, then remove any others to leave the spurs well spaced and uncongested.

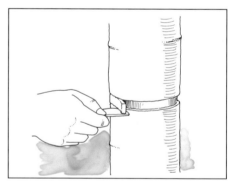

2 Carefully remove the bark with the knife blade (use the blunt side to lift it), right around the tree.

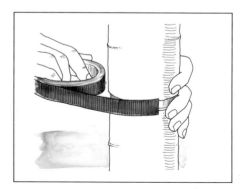

3 Wind a waterproof tape around the wound several times to reduce the risk of infection while the wound is healing. Remove when the wound has healed.

PRUNING A TIP BEARER

1 Some varieties of apple bear their fruit mainly at the ends of the branches instead of on clusters of spurs. Spur pruning is unsuitable for these.

Simply shorten sideshoots that are longer than 23cm (9in) by cutting them back to five or six buds. Do not prune sideshoots shorter than 23cm (9in).

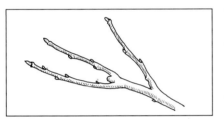

2 To avoid overcrowded branches, thin out any groups of very vigorous young shoots that have grown close together.

3 If there are badly placed or crossing branches, cut out some of them to keep the tree open and uncluttered.

NICKING AND NOTCHING

If the growth of a shoot is too vigorous, you can reduce it by removing a small crescent of bark and cambium layer (cut until you reach the hard wood), just *below* a bud. This will restrict the growth of the shoot above. This process is called nicking.

If you want to stimulate a branch to grow out, perhaps to fill in a gap, make a similar cut just *above* the bud. This is known as notching (above).

Apples grown on dwarfing rootstocks will make compact bushes or small trees, like this 'Sunset'. Ask your nursery or garden centre for advice about the likely sizes of the trees on the rootstocks available.

THINNING AND ROOT PRUNING

To grow large apples and pears, thin overcrowded spurs in winter and thin overcrowded fruits in summer. If your fruit tree is too vigorous, you may be able to restrict its size by root pruning.

ROOT PRUNING

1 A fruit tree on a suitable rootstock should not require root pruning, but if you inherit a tree that's too large, root pruning when the tree is dormant may help to reduce its vigour. Make an arc around half of the tree, just inside the spread of the branches. Root prune only one half of the tree – do the other side the following year.

2 Excavate a trench around half the tree, following the guide line marked.

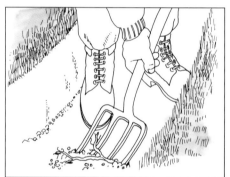

3 Use a fork to expose deeper roots without damaging the fine fibrous ones.

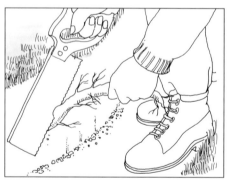

4 Saw through the large exposed roots, but leave as many smaller fibrous roots as possible undamaged. Finally, return the soil to the trench and firm it.

THINNING SPURS

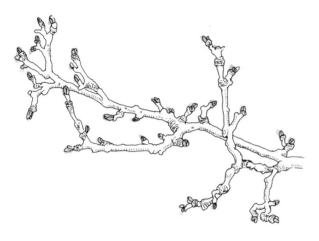

1 Thinning overcrowded spurs on apples and pears will help the tree produce fewer but better fruits. Remove those spurs growing on the underside of the branch first.

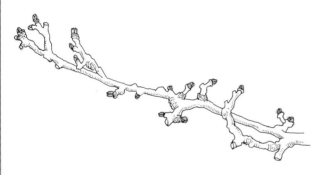

2 Remove the most congested and the weakest spurs to leave the remaining ones well spaced.

THINNING FRUIT

1 If you leave densely packed branches like this unthinned, the fruit will be small and of poor quality. Thin them so that you have less fruit but of better quality.

2 Use secateurs to remove surplus fruits, leaving those that remain about 5–8cm (2–3in) apart.

PROTECTING YOUR FRUIT

Apples and pears are prone to many pests and diseases, so some spraying is advisable if you want a good, unblemished crop. However, by using some non-toxic controls, and spraying at a time when the chemicals are effective but not likely to harm beneficial insects, you can usually strike a balance between fruit protection and concern for the environment.

GREASE BANDING

1 The wingless females of winter moths (the caterpillars of which cause much damage to apples) climb the fruit trees in late autumn or early winter (sometimes in early spring). A grease band will trap them and reduce the population. Applying grease is a messy job, so buy proprietary grease bands. Cut off enough to go around the trunk, with a short overlap.

2 Tie the bands into place at the top and bottom. Make sure that they are in close contact with the trunk.

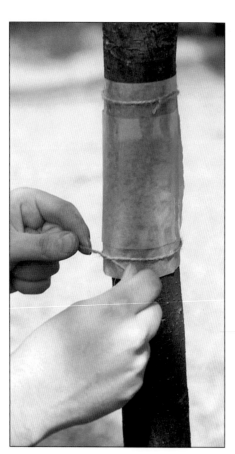

3 Pull off the protective cover from the middle of the band, to expose the sticky greased surface. Check periodically to make sure the grease has not been bridged by fallen leaves.

PHEROMONE TRAPS

1 Pheromone traps work by attracting male insects to the scent of a female. They are available for codling moths and a few other insects. Assemble the traps as recommended by the manufacturer.

2 Place the pheromone (usually contained in a sort of pellet) on the sticky surface of the trap.

3 Hang the trap in the fruit tree, within easy reach so it will be easy to check regularly. The sticky surface of the trap will catch and kill many males, and this alone will reduce the population if fewer females are fertilized. You can also use the traps as a guide to the best time to spray – check the traps twice a week, and spray when there seem to be a lot of males around.

TERMS YOU MAY NEED TO KNOW

Many sprays are applied in the spring to control pests and diseases on apples and pears, but it is important not to use them when bees are pollinating the flowers. Make sure you understand the following terms, which spray instructions may include.
Bud burst is when tight buds are just expanding, **green cluster** when the flower buds are obvious but still green, **pink bud** (white bud for pears) is when colour starts to show, and **petal fall** is when the petals of the first flowers start to drop.

pink bud (apple)

full flower

How To Grow Outdoor Grapes

There are several ways to grow outdoor grapes, but the Guyot system described here is one of the easiest. If you are starting from scratch with a new vine, follow the advice on formative training.

Formative Pruning

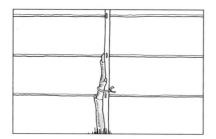

1 After planting, prune the main shoot back to leave just three strong buds.

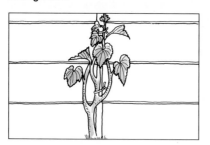

2 In the first summer, let the three shoots grow, and tie them to the support so that they grow vertically.

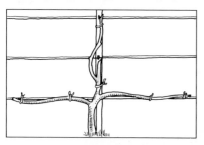

3 In the next winter, lower the two strongest shoots and tie them horizontally to the bottom wire. Then shorten the ends to leave each one about 75cm (2½ft) long. Finally, cut the remaining upright shoot back to leave three buds. The following summer tie in the shoots that grow vertically from the horizontal shoots, as described for established pruning.

Established Guyot Pruning

1 Prune the central shoot back to leave three buds. Select two new shoots to shorten and tie in, and cut out the others flush with the main stump.

2 Bend over the two young shoots that have been retained, and tie these to the bottom wires.

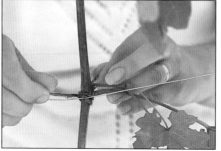 

3 During the spring and summer new shoots will grow from the branches tied to the bottom wire. Tie these in to the other wires so that they grow vertically.

4 Pinch out the growing tips two leaves above the top wire, and also pinch out any sideshoots that grow from shoots already carrying fruit.

Grapes can be very decorative in fruit. This variety is 'Brandt'.

How To Grow Peaches And Nectarines

Peaches and nectarines are both treated in the same way. A fan-trained tree is likely to give the best results in all but mild areas, but the early formative training is complicated, so it is best to buy a ready-trained tree or to consult a specialist book for instructions. The advice given here is for established bush and fan trees.

Thinning

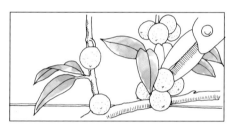

Peaches and nectarines may need thinning to encourage the production of bigger and better fruit. Snip off surplus fruit with secateurs, to leave just one fruit per cluster. It may be necessary to thin again later, to leave the fruits about 15cm (6in) apart.

Pruning A Bush Tree

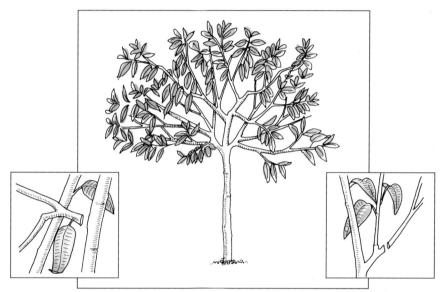

1 In early summer, cut out any dead, diseased or badly crossing branches. If parts of the tree have become congested, cut out some of the oldest branches.

2 If the tree has been fruiting for several years, cut back any branches that are dying back at the tip. Take them back to healthy wood where there is a young replacement shoot. Do the same for any old branches that are now fruiting poorly – but don't do this to more than one-quarter of the branches overall.

Pruning A Fan Tree

1 When the leaves are beginning to emerge in the spring, disbud the young shoots to leave sideshoots to grow about every 15cm (6in). Always leave the bud at the base of the shoot untouched, as this will form a replacement shoot to carry fruit the following year.

2 After the fruit has been harvested, prune each shoot that has borne fruit back to a suitable replacement. This is usually a shoot that has developed from a bud left to grow from the base during spring thinning.

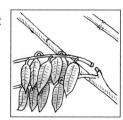

3 Tie this replacement shoot to the cane that supported the fruited shoot that has just been removed.

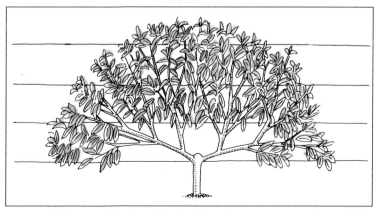

HOW TO GROW CURRANTS

Blackcurrants are easy to grow and prune. Red and white currants are also easy fruit to grow, but they are trained and pruned in a different way.

PLANTING

1 Plant in well-prepared ground to which fertilizer has been added. Plant at the original depth.

2 Plant 1.2–1.5m (4–5ft) apart and firm the soil well around the roots.

3 Immediately after planting (or the following winter if planting when the shoots are not dormant), cut back all the stems on a blackcurrant to the first or second bud above the ground. This will stimulate more shoots to grow from the base of the plant.

4 Red and white currants are treated differently. After planting (or the next spring if not planting during the dormant season), prune off any sideshoots growing within 10–15cm (4–6in) of the soil, to produce a clear single stem (a leg) at the base.

5 Reduce the length of each main shoot by about half, pruning to an outward-facing bud. In the subsequent winter, reduce the length of all the main shoots that have grown from last year's pruning by about half.

PRUNING AN ESTABLISHED BUSH

1 Prune blackcurrant bushes over three years old on an annual basis, ideally after harvesting or in the autumn. Cut any low-growing, badly placed or crossing branches back to their point of origin.

2 Prune established red and white currant bushes annually, in winter or early spring. Shorten the tips of the leading shoots (the longest branches) by 5–8cm (2–3in) to encourage further branching.

3 Prune each sideshoot from these branches back to just one bud.

Raspberries, Blackberries And Hybrid Berries

Planting Raspberries

1 Plant raspberries about 45cm (1½ft) apart in a shallow trench on well-prepared ground that has had plenty of compost or rotted manure incorporated. Spread out the roots before returning the plant to the soil.

2 Tread the soil firmly around the plant. Then cut the cane back to about 25cm (10in). In mid summer, cut the original stem back to just above the ground. Then tie in the new canes to the support wires.

Pruning And Training Raspberries

1 To make pruning and harvesting easy, train to wires stretched between posts. Space the wire about 30cm (1ft) apart.

2 Prune summer-flowering varieties after fruiting has finished. Cut canes that have fruited back to ground level. Leave the younger, paler canes unpruned. Prune autumn-fruiting varieties during the winter or in early spring before new growth starts. Cut *all* the canes back to ground level.

Pruning Blackberries And Hybrid Berries

1 To make pruning and harvesting easy, always train to wires stretched between stout posts. Space the wires about 30cm (1ft) apart.

2 Prune an established plant after fruiting or during the dormant season. Cut out all those canes that have fruited, taking them back close to the ground. Tie in the new shoots, moving them across the wires to space them out.

Planting Blackberries And Hybrid Berries

Plant bare-rooted plants when they are dormant – from late autumn to early spring – spacing them 2.4–5m (8–15ft) apart, depending on the vigour of the variety.

How To Train Raspberries

There are several ways to train raspberries, but a post and rail system like the one illustrated above is simple and effective.

Space the wires at heights of about 75cm (2½ft), 90cm (3ft) and 1.5m (5ft). Tie in the new shoots each season when they are about 90cm (3ft) tall. Space them about 10cm (4in) apart.

By the end of the season the canes will be taller than the top wire. Bend them over and tie them down to the top wire. In spring cut back all the tips to leave the canes about 15cm (6in) above the top wire.

HOW TO GROW GOOSEBERRIES

Plant, feed and mulch gooseberries
as for blackcurrants, but prune
after planting as described below.

FORMATIVE PRUNING

After planting (or in the following winter if
not planted during the dormant season),
prune back the shoots by about half. This
will stimulate plenty of branching.

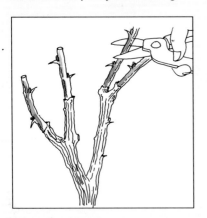

PRUNING AN ESTABLISHED BUSH

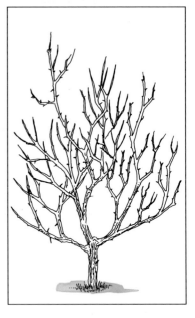

1 Prune bushes over
three years old on an
annual basis. Do this in
the winter or early
spring. Shorten the tips
of all the main shoots by
about half of the growth
made during the summer
– or to within three or
four buds of the old
growth if you find this
easier.

2 Prune each sideshoot from these
branches back to about 8cm (3in).

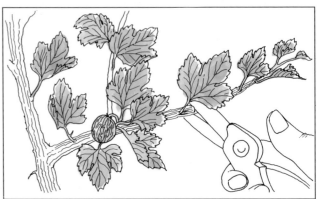

3 In early to mid summer cut sideshoots
back to about five leaves from their
base. This is not essential but will keep the
bush more open and reduce the risk of
diseases becoming a problem. Leave the
tips of the main shoots intact during
summer pruning.

HOW TO GROW STRAWBERRIES

Strawberries are very easy to grow, but to be sure of good crops always buy certified disease-free plants. If your plants begin to deteriorate through diseases, don't propagate your own but buy fresh plants. The method described below is simple and reliable. Bear in mind that some varieties crop just once in early or mid summer, while others described as 'perpetual' or 'ever-bearing' varieties produce several crops between early summer and mid autumn.

PLANTING

Strawberries need fertile soil. Work plenty of garden compost or rotten manure into the ground and prepare a weed-free bed for planting.

Rake in a balanced garden fertilizer, then plant about 45cm (18in) apart in rows 75cm (30in) apart.

Strawberry plants sometimes arrive with bare roots. Spread the roots out on a mound, and make sure the crown is level with the surrounding surface. Return soil.

Most strawberries are sold in pots. Water them an hour before planting, then knock out of the pot and plant at their original depth.

Remove any flowers that appear during the first year, if they were planted in the autumn or spring. This will ensure the plants become well established before having to carry a crop of fruit. Let them fruit if planted the previous summer.

ROUTINE CARE

1 Strawberries benefit from regular feeding. Apply sulphate of potash at the rate of 20g/sq m (½oz/sq yd) in early spring.
If the plants look as though their growth needs a boost, apply sulphate of ammonia at the same rate in mid spring.

2 Keep down weeds by regular hoeing or hand weeding.

3 Keep the fruit clean by using special mats. These must be in position at least by the time the plant starts to develop fruit.

NEW PLANTS FROM RUNNERS

In early or mid summer, spread out the runners that form and peg the small stem where there is a strong tuft of leaves into pots of compost plunged into the soil. Hold the runner in contact with the soil with a piece of bent wire.

Pinch or cut off the runner just beyond the pegged-down point, but *do not sever the link with the parent plant.* Remove surplus runners not required for propagation.

Check after about six weeks, and if the plant has rooted well, sever it from its parent.

4 If you have a lot of strawberries, it may be cheaper and more convenient to lay straw down around the plants instead of using individual mats. Lift the leaves and fruit to lay the straw thickly between soil and developing fruits.

HARVESTING AND STORING FRUIT

Fruit needs picking with special care if you plan to store or preserve it. Store only perfect fruit – you should use up damaged or imperfect fruits while they are still fresh.

HOW TO STORE

These are some of the best ways to store some of the most popular fruits. There are, of course, variations on the methods suggested and if in doubt you should consult an authoritative cookery book.

APPLES	Store wrapped; freeze as slices or purée; bottle as slices
APRICOTS	Freeze halved; bottle
BLACKBERRIES	Freeze whole; bottle
CHERRIES	Freeze after stoning (pitting); bottle
CURRANTS (BLACK, RED, WHITE)	Freeze whole (blackcurrants may also be frozen as purée); bottle
GOOSEBERRIES	Freeze whole after topping and tailing, or as purée; bottle
PEACHES AND NECTARINES	Freeze soon after stoning (pitting) – they discolour quickly; bottle after stoning
PEARS	Store wrapped
PLUMS	Freeze after stoning (pitting); bottle
RASPBERRIES	Freeze whole; bottle
STRAWBERRIES	Freeze whole (not very satisfactory) or as purée

PICKING AND STORING SOFT FRUIT

1 Pick strawberries carefully by the stalk to avoid bruising.

2 Pick raspberries regularly as they become ripe. Pull them gently off the stalk so that the plug or core within the fruit remains behind on the stalk (pick with the stalk only if you intend to exhibit them in a show).

3 Most soft fruit freezes well, though strawberries are often disappointing. Remove any stalks and hulls, then freeze the fruit whole, spaced out on trays.

4 As soon as it is frozen, transfer the fruit to bags or boxes, excluding as much air as possible.

1 Apples and pears are ready for picking when the fruit comes away from the tree easily without breaking the stalk. Cup the fruit in the palm of your hand and give it a very slight twist. Remove with the stalk intact.

2 Bruised fruit does not store well. Line a basket with straw or crumpled paper, and gently place the fruit in this as you harvest it.

3 Wrap each fruit individually in greaseproof paper (or newspaper, at a pinch). Start by placing the fruit in the centre of a square of paper.

4 Fold two opposite corners over the fruit, handling it carefully.

5 Fold over the other two corners and place the fruit in trays with the loose end held by the weight of the fruit.

6 **RIGHT** Place in wooden slatted boxes or trays, or in some other well-ventilated container, and keep undisturbed in a cool but frost-free place.

FRUIT & VEGETABLES

245

FRUIT FACTS AT YOUR FINGERTIPS

Use this table as a quick reference guide for advice on the requirements and harvesting times for all the common fruits. The dates given are for the most popular varieties and methods of cultivation: these may vary for specific varieties or techniques and, of course, the weather. Always check the label or ask the nurseryman for planting instructions, spacings and details such as suitable pollinators where these are required.

NAME	SOIL AND SITE	HARVEST	REMARKS
APPLE	Undemanding regarding soil. Full sun. Avoid frost pockets	Late summer to late autumn, depending on variety	Regular pruning and spraying usually necessary for good crops. Some varieties need pollinators. Choose a dwarfing rootstock for a small garden
APRICOT	Needs well-drained soil and a warm, sunny position. Frost protection for flowers is important	Mid and late summer	For a small garden choose a tree grafted on a very dwarfing rootstock. Water freely in dry weather. Can be grown as a bush, but except in the mildest areas fans are more suitable
BLACKBERRY AND HYBRID BERRIES	Undemanding	Mid summer to early autumn, depending on variety	Regular pruning and training are essential to prevent canes becoming untidy and difficult to control
BLACKCURRANT	Undemanding, but avoid frost pockets or grow late varieties	Mid and late summer	Protection from birds may be necessary. Annual pruning and feeding are beneficial
BLUEBERRY	Suitable only for acid soils – pH 5.5 or lower	Mid to late summer	Protection from birds may be necessary. Plant two varieties to ensure good pollination
CHERRY	Ordinary soil. Acid cherries tolerate shade, but sweet cherries need full sun	Mid and late summer	To make cherry growing easy in a small garden, choose a self-fertile variety (no pollinator is needed), grafted on to a very dwarfing rootstock
FIG	Undemanding regarding soil, but grow in a warm, sunny position, perhaps trained against a wall	Late summer and early autumn	It may be necessary to restrict root spread. Best grown against a wall in cool areas, where winter protection of young shoots and immature fruits is also important. Protect ripening fruits from birds
GOOSEBERRY	Undemanding regarding soil. Best in full sun, but will tolerate partial shade. Avoid frost pockets	Early and mid summer	Very prone to a form of mildew, so routine spraying may be necessary. Can be grown as a cordon against a wall or fence where space is limited
GRAPE	Well-drained, fertile soil. Full sun	Early and mid autumn	Dessert grapes are best grown in a greenhouse, but take up a lot of space. Many outdoor varieties can be used as dessert grapes or for wine. Annual pruning is important

NAME	SOIL AND SITE	HARVEST	REMARKS
KIWI	Undemanding regarding soil, but a warm, sunny position is important	Mid autumn	Needs a male plant to pollinate the female fruiting variety. Requires a lot of space and strong support for the climbing stems. Not suitable for cold areas. Harvest before the first frost
PEACH AND NECTARINE	Fertile soil, sunny position. Avoid frost pockets and provide a sheltered position	Mid summer to early autumn, depending on variety	Except in the warmest areas, best grown as a fan against a warm wall (regular pruning essential). Can be grown in a large pot if the rootstock is very dwarfing (take indoors to protect blossom if necessary)
PEAR	Fertile soil and warm, sunny position	Early autumn to early winter	Will need a pollinator. Seek advice for your variety unless there are already plenty of pears in the neighbourhood. Can be unreliable in cold areas (seek local advice about varieties)
PLUM, GAGE, DAMSON	Fertile soil and a sunny position. Avoid frost pockets	Late summer to late autumn	Avoid early varieties in cold areas (blossom is often damaged by frost). Some varieties need a pollinator (seek advice when buying). For a small garden be sure to buy a tree grown on a dwarfing rootstock
RASPBERRY	Fertile soil and a sunny position	Mid summer to mid autumn, depending on variety	Prune and train annually (the methods differ according to whether the variety is summer-fruiting or autumn-fruiting). To spread the season, choose a selection of summer- and autumn-fruiting varieties
RED CURRANT AND WHITE CURRANT	Undemanding regarding soil if well-drained, but need a sheltered spot in full sun or partial shade	Mid and late summer	Can be trained as a cordon if space is limited
STRAWBERRY	Fertile soil in full sun	Early summer to autumn, depending on variety	Propagate new plants regularly and replant the strawberry bed every couple of years as old plants deteriorate

SUPPLIERS

UK

GARDEN EQUIPMENT AND SUPPLIES

Axminster Power Tool Centre
Chard Street
Axminster
Devon EX13 5DZ
Tel: 0297 33656
Fax: 0297 35242

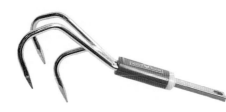

Chase Organics (GB) Ltd
(fertilizers)
Coombelands House
Addlestone
Weybridge
Surrey KT15 1HY
Tel: 0932 820958

Greevale Farm Ltd
(Fisons Origins Range)
Wonastow Road
Monmouth
Gwent NP5 3XX

Humber Fertilisers
PO Box 27
Stoneferry
Hull
Humberside HU8 8DQ

Jemp Engineering Ltd
(soil warming cable)
Canal Estate
Station Road
Langley
Berkshire SL3 6EG

P G Horticulture
(modules)
Street Farm
Thornham Magna
Eye
Suffolk IP23 8HB

SEEDS

B & T World Seeds
Whitenell House
Fiddington
Bridgwater
Somerset TA5 1JE

D T Brown & Co Ltd
Station Road
Poulton-le-Fylde
Blackpool
Lancashire FY6 7HX
Tel: 0253 882371

Chase Organics (GB) Ltd
(see Garden Equipment and Supplies)

Chiltern Seeds
Bortree Stile
Ulverston
Cumbria LA12 7PB
Tel: 0229 581137

Cowcombe Farm Herbs
Gipsy Lane
Chalford
Stroud
Gloucestershire GL6 8HP

Samuel Dobie & Sons Ltd
Broomhill Way
Torquay
Devon TQ2 7QW
Tel: 0803 616281

King Crown Quality Seeds
Monks Farm
Pantling Lane
Coggleshall Road
Kelvedon
Essex CO5 9PG

W Robinson & Sons Ltd
Sunny Bank
Forton
Nr Preston
Lancashire PR3 0BN
Tel: 0524 791210

Seeds by Size
70 Varney Road
Hemel Hempstead
Hertfordshire HP1 1TB

Seymour's Selected Seeds
Abacus House
Station Yard
Needham Market
Suffolk IP6 8AS

Stewart's (Nottingham) Ltd
3 George Street
Nottingham
NG1 3BH
Tel: 0602 476338

NURSERIES

Country Park Nursery
Essex Gardens
Hornchurch
Essex RM11 3BU
Tel: 0708 447643

Craigieburn Classic Plants
Craigieburn House
by Moffat
Dumfriesshire DG10 9LF
Tel: 056 386286

Crankan Nurseries
New Mill
Penzance
Cornwall

Hazeldene Nursery
Dean Street
East Farleigh
Maidstone
Kent ME15 0PS

The Herb Nursery
Grange Farm
Main Street
Thistleton
Rutland LE15 7RE
Tel: 0572 767658

Holden Clough Nursery
Holden
Bolton by Bowland
Nr Clitheroe
Lancashire BB7 4PF
Tel: 0200 447615

Marle Place Plants and Gardens
Marle Place
Brenchley
Nr Tonbridge
Kent TN12 7HS

Naked Cross Nurseries
Waterloo Road
Corfe Mullen
Wimborne
Dorset BH21 3SR
Tel: 0202 693256

Old Manor Nurseries
South Leverton
Retford
Nottinghamshire DN22 0BX

Pennine Nurseries
Shelley
Huddersfield
Yorkshire HD8 8LG
Tel: 0484 605511

The Plant Place
63/67 Camberwell Road
London SE5 8TR
Tel: 071-252 6565

Pocock's Nurseries
Dandys Ford Lane
Sherfield English
Romsey
Hampshire SO51 6FT
Tel: 0794 23514

Rumwood Nurseries
Langley
Maidstone
Kent ME17 3ND
Tel: 0622 861477

St Bridget Nurseries Ltd
Old Rydon Lane
Exeter
Devon EX2 7JY
Tel: 0392 873672

Stillingfleet Lodge Nurseries
Stillingfleet
Yorkshire YO4 6HW

Stydd Nursery
Stonygate Lane
Ribchester
Nr Preston
Lancashire PR3 3YN
Tel: 0254 878 797

Sussex County Gardens
Newhaven Road
Kingston
Nr Lewes
E Sussex BN7 3NE

Thyme House Nursery
Manea March
Cambridgeshire
Tel: 0354 680412

Walter Blom & Son Ltd
Coombelands Nurseries
Leavesdon
Watford
Hertfordshire WD2 7BH

Weasdale Nurseries
Kirkby Stephen
Cumbria CA17 4LX
Tel: 05396 23246

The Wildflower Centre
Church Farm
Sisland
Loddon
Norwich
Norfolk NR14 6EF

Wyevale Nurseries Ltd
Kings Acre
Hereford & Worcester HR4 7AY
Tel: 0432 352255

GARDEN STRUCTURES AND ORNAMENTS

Agriframes Ltd
Charlwoods Road
East Grinstead
W Sussex RH19 2HG

Capital Garden Products Ltd
Hurst Green
Etchingham
E Sussex TN19 7QU
Tel: 0580 201092

PONDS AND FOUNTAINS

JNS
21 Greenside
Prestwood
Buckinghamshire HP16 0SE

Pondliners
Freepost 62
Nicolson Link
Clifton Moor
York YO1 1SS
Tel: 0904 691169
Fax: 0904 691133

Reef Aquatics
Catfoot Lane
Lambley
Nottinghamshire NG4 4QG
Tel: 0602 676100
Fax: 0602 673266

Stapeley Water Gardens Ltd
London Road
Nantwich
Cheshire
Tel: 0270 628111

The Very Interesting Rock Company
PO Box 27
Leamington Spa
Warwickshire CV32 5GR
Tel: 0926 313465

COMPOST BIN MANUFACTURERS

Border Composting Systems
The Skenchill
Welsh Newton
Monmouth
Gwent NP5 3QJ

Original Organics Ltd
Organic House
PO Box 16
Cullompton
Devon EX15 2YZ
Tel: 0884 7681

FENCING

Lemar
Harrowbrook Industrial Estate
Hinckley
Leicestershire LE10 3DJ
Tel: 0455 637077

M C Products
Home Farm Cliffe
Piercebridge
Darlington
Co Durham DL2 3SS

Rob Turner
Unit 16
Moore's Yard
High Street
Stalham
Norfolk NR12 9AN
Tel: 0692 580091

GREENHOUSES, SUNROOMS AND CONSERVATORIES

Alispeed Ltd
Unit B4
Hortonwood 10
Telford
Shropshire TF1 4ES

Alite Metals
7 Maze Street
Barton Hill
Bristol BS5 9TE
Tel: 0272 553100

Archwood Greenhouses
Robinwood
Goodrich
Herefordshire HR9 6HT
Tel: 0600 890125

Regal National Garden Building Centre
Cromford Road
Langley Mill
Nottinghamshire NG16 4EB
Tel: 0773 530428

AUSTRALIA

GARDEN CENTRES

Swanes
490 Galston Rd
Dural NSW 2158
Tel: (02) 651 1322
Fax: (02) 651 2146

Michele Shennen's
Garden Centres
44 Old Barrenjoey Rd
Avalon NSW 2107
Tel: (02) 918 6738

Bonds Nursery
363 Military Rd
Mosman NSW 2088
Tel: (02) 953 3700
Fax: (02) 486 3323

Sherringhams Nurseries Pty Ltd
299a Lane Cove Rd
North Ryde NSW 2113
Tel: (02) 888 3133
Fax: (02) 805 1823

Rast Brothers
29 Kissing Point Rd
Turramurra NSW 2074
Tel: (02) 44 2134

Tropigro
PO Box 39827
Winnellie NT 0821
Tel: (089) 84 3200

Gardenway Nurseries
269 Monier Road
Darra QLD 4076

Perrots Nursery
71 Elkhorn Street
Enoggera QLD 4051
Tel: (07) 355 7700

Gippsland Growers
125 Sutton St
Warragul VIC 3920
Tel/Fax: (056) 23 6718

Warner's Nurseries Pty Ltd
395 Warrigal Rd
Burwood VIC 3125
Tel: (03) 808 2321

Wattleview Gardens
32 Wattletree Rd
Ferntree Gully VIC 3156
Tel: (03) 758 6449

Richgro Horticultural Products
Lot 186 Acourt Rd
Canningvale WA 6155
Tel: (09) 455 1323
Fax: (09) 455 1297

SEEDS

Australian Seed Company
(Australian native tree and shrub seeds)
5 Rosedale Ave
Hazelbrook NSW 2779
Tel: (047) 58 6132

Ellison Horticultural
(tree, shrub and palm seed)
PO Box 365
Nowra NSW 2541
Tel: (044) 21 4255
Fax: (044) 23 0859

Harvest Seed Company
(wholesale native and exotic seed &
seedling suppliers)
PO Box 544
Newport Beach NSW 2106
Tel: (02) 997 2277
Fax: (02) 997 6924

Diggers Seeds
Box 300
Dromana VIC 3936
Tel: (059) 87 1877

NEW ZEALAND

NURSERIES

Big Trees
Main Road
Coatesville
Auckland
Tel: (09) 415-9983

Golden Coast Nurseries
Main Road
North Paekakariki
Tel: 292-8556
Fax: 292-8556

Kent's Nurseries
Cr. Fergusson Drive & Ranfurly Street
Trentham
Tel: (4) 528-3889

Rainbow Tree Nursery
Cooper Road
Ramarama
Sth. Auckland

GARDENING CENTRES

California Green World Garden Centre
139 Park Road
Miramar
Wellington
Tel: (04) 388-3260
Fax: (04) 388-4820

Palmers Garden World
Cr. Shore & Orakei Roads
Remuera
Auckland
Tel: (09) 524 4038

Plantarama Garden Centre
104 State Highway 16
Massy
Auckland

Zeniths
92 Epuni Street
Lower Hutt
Tel: (04) 566-1493

GARDEN POOL CENTRES

Garden Statues and Ornaments
Hewletts Road
Mt Maunganui
Tel: (07) 575-5797
Fax: (07) 552-5244

Jansen's Pet Centre
985 Mt Eden Road
Three Kings
Auckland
Tel: (09) 625-7915

STATUARY

Ornamentally Yours
12 Princess Street
Onehunga
Auckland
Tel: (09) 634-4305
Fax: (09) 622-1029

Garden Statues and Ornaments
(see Garden Pool Centres)

GAZEBOS

Wellington Sheds & Carports
Cr. Petone Esplanade & Hutt Road
Petone
Wellington
Tel: (04) 568-9626

INDEX

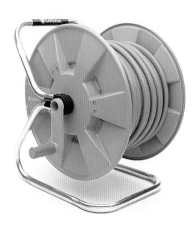

R

S

T

U

V

W